THE INDEPENDENT GUIDE TO DUBAI 2017

Limit of Liability and Disclaimer of Warranty:
The publisher has used its best efforts in preparing this book, and the information provided herein is provided "as is." Independent Guides and the author make no representation or warranties with respect to the accuracy or completeness of the contents of this book and specifically disclaims any implied warranties of merchantability or fitness for any particular purpose and shall in no event be liable for any loss of profit or any other commercial damage, including but not limited to special, incidental, consequential, or other damages.

Please read all signs before entering attractions, as well as the terms and conditions of any third party companies used. Prices are approximate, and do fluctuate.

Table of Contents

Introduction

Located on the Persian golf and the most populous city in the United Arab Emirates, Dubai has in recent years become a must-visit location.

Home to the Burj Khalifa - the tallest building in the world - Dubai has become an overnight success and *the* place to be for the super-rich. From iconic hotels such as the Burj Al Arab to the entirely artificial Palm Islands, extravagance is abound in this megalopolis.

Dubai is often thought to be a city funded by the sale and trade of oil but, while in the past this may have been true, today less than 5% of the emirate's revenue comes from oil.

This is far from being a soulless place to visit either, amongst all the shopping malls and resorts lies an interesting and rich history that is just begging to be explored. We make sure to highlight these unique locations in this guide.

Plus, despite all the wealth and extravagance, there are still many affordable and enjoyable activities to take part in. Accommodation and dining are varied both in price and taste too.

This travel guide explores this unique location that welcomes western travelers, yet caters to a local, conservative viewpoint.

Throughout this guide you will discover what lies in the many neighbourhoods of the city, get an insight into the local culture and gain practical information to make your visit hassle-free.

Dubai: A Brief History

To understand this emirate, we must first take a look at how it all began - before all the skyscrapers were around, Dubai was a very different place.

Home to some of the most iconic buildings, Dubai has become known as the modern day crossroads connecting the east and west. The city has grown to become a global leader of smart city design and ultimately one of the most connected and visited city's in the world.

However, despite the surge in popularity of Dubai in the modern day, it wasn't always that way. Just 200 years ago, Dubai was a small fishing settlement with a population of 1,200 people.

The Bani Yas Tribe

The tribe were traditionally one of the biggest and most respected throughout the whole of Arabia, and by far the biggest and most powerful tribe in the UAE. They were of such a numerical advantage and possessed vast military prowess, that they were often targeted by other tribes for protection from threats. The tribe often settled in locations of prominence.

In 1833, there were to be some major changes to the rulership of Dubai when the Maktoum dynasty of the tribe took over from the Abu Falasa clan. The transition was relatively peaceful and meant that Dubai became a different Sheikdom from Abu Dhabir.

On taking over Dubai, the Maktoum Dynasty consisted of approximately 800 members. Today, almost 200 years on, the Maktoum dynasty still act as the ruling family of Dubai with Sheikh Mohammed bin Rashid Al Maktoum having ruled the emirate since 2006.

British influence and the Trucial States

At the beginning of the year in 1835, the ruler of Dubai came to an agreement with the British government and signed the General Maritime Peace Treaty which saw the start of a British influence in the region.

The treaty was signed in order to curb the excessive plundering and piracy within the area and was also the first official denunciation of the slave trade throughout the world.

In response to the signed truce, the British additionally agreed to stay out of the administration of Dubai.

A second treaty with the British
In 1892, after a successful relationship, the Trucial Sheikhdoms and the British government signed another treaty which further established closer ties between the two sides. After seeing the intentions of other European countries, the British sought a response and the signing of the treaty was very much the perfect response from the British government.

The deal was similar to deals already in place between the British and other Persian Gulf territories and it further strengthened their stranglehold in the region.

In return to the British promise of protection of the Trucial sealine from any external threat and the promise of support for land attacks, ruling Sheikhs agreed to commit themselves and their land solely to Great Britain. This included not giving up any of their land to anyone except Great Britain and also ensured they wouldn't form any relationship with foreign powers apart from Great Britain without the consent from the British government.

The treaty, which was named 'The Exclusive Agreement' was signed by all members of the Trucial Sheikhdoms and made official in March of 1892.

Economic Depression
In the decade post 1930, disaster struck Dubai due to the collapse of the previously booming pearling industry. The economic effects of the faltering pearling industry were followed by The Great Depression.

The aftermath hit the population of Dubai with devastating effects as the depression led to a mass starvation which ultimately resulted in residents fleeing to other Persian Gulf territories such as Abu Dhabi.

Border dispute with Abu Dhabi
The 1940s saw Dubai experience a dispute with Persian neighbors Abu Dhabi over the border in the northern part of the emirate and resulted in war.

The fighting only ended with a small number of deaths but it required an intervention from the British army who created a buffer frontier along the disputed border which resulted in a temporary ceasefire.

The two Emirates only fully settled the dispute 30 years later in 1979.

A new power
1958 saw Sheikh Rashid bin Saeed Al Maktoum take over power. He is largely credited for the ambitious expansion plans that made Dubai a force in the Persian Gulf.

One of the biggest accelerators was the discovery of oil in the area which would allow for the financial resources to implement such large scale plans.

However, even before the discovery of oil in 1966, the ruler was already on the way to creating something special and leaving his mark on the city. With revenue from trading activities, the ruler had enough financial resources to initiate the construction of important and efficient infrastructure.

The creation of such infrastructure allowed for electricity to be introduced to the city for the first time, which in turn allowed for the initiation of telephone services.

The construction of such essential infrastructure really allowed for the city to develop and soon after, Rashid Al Maktoum signed off plans to build an airport.

The discovery of oil

In 1966, oil was discovered in territorial waters just off mainland Dubai. The find was of monumental news to the ruling Sheikh who could finally realize his ambitions of a greater Dubai.

However, despite the initial discovery, the quantity of oil actually discovered was shown to be in much smaller numbers than their neighbors over in Abu Dhabi. Nonetheless, Rashid Al Maktoum granted concessions to international oil companies to proceed with the nurturing of the oil.

The decision by the ruler to allow for these companies to enter the area to work was followed by a huge influx of foreign workers predominantly from India and Bangladesh, which ultimately saw the city's population grow by an unprecedented 300% between the late 1960's and 1975.

The first oil field was constructed in the Jebel Ali area located just outside of modern day Dubai. The oil field became locally known as a Fateh and is an important factor in the success of Dubai today.

The discovery of oil in the area also led to the construction of large storage tanks locally known as a 'Kazzan' across the Jebel Ali area. The 'Kazzan's' were built by a company called Chicago Bridge and Iron which had such an influence on the city that the ruler decided to name a beach after them (Chicago Beach), which stood until 1997 when it was renamed Jumeirah Beach.

The influence of Sheikh Rashid Al Maktoum
Much of Dubai's current day success and popularity is credited to ruler Rashid Al Maktoum's decision to diversifying the trading economy, in addition to oil revenue. This ensure a long term economic success even after Dubai's oil reserves run out.

Examples of this include the creation of Port Rashid, the construction of an extensive road network, and modern schools and hospitals.

The formation of The United Arab Emirates Federation
In 1968, British Prime Minister Harold Wilson stated his intentions to withdraw troops and dealing with the area's foreign policy.

Britain gave three years notice of their decision with an intention to withdraw in 1971, which they duly did.

Dubai and Abu Dhabi entered negotiations, along with four other emirate states including Sharjah, Ajman, Umm Al Qawain and Fuljairah to form a federation by the name of the United Arab Emirates. A seventh emirate, Ras Al Khaimah joined a few years later to complete the modern day United Arab Emirates.

One of the major agreements between the emirate states was that both Dubai and Abu Dhabi would hold the greater proportion of control over the country with both cities being the only Emirates to hold veto power over situations of great importance.

Two years after the formation of the federation, Dubai and the other members adopted the UAE dirham as a uniform currency.

Persian Gulf War
1990 saw the death of Sheikh Rashid Al Maktoum, but also saw the outbreak of the Persian Gulf War between the coalition forces of the United States of America, Great Britain, Saudi Arabia, France against Saddam Hussein's Iraq.

Although not directly involved, Dubai as part of the UAE played a key role in providing military aid to the coalition forces. The war had a major impact on the local economy of Dubai which severely stunted growth as investors withdrew money and trade from the city.

The instability of the economy wasn't to last for long, however, and during the mid 90s, the economy grew once again with a large

number of foreign traders, especially from Kuwait and Bahrain, moving their operations and business interests to Dubai.

In 2003 during the allies invasion of Iraq, Dubai again offered the allied forces resources in the name of strategic refueling bases.

Elaborate architecture and rapid expansion

Within the last 20 years, Dubai has really started to take off on a number of fronts. With the infrastructure originally being put in place during Sheikh Rashid Al Maktoums reign prior to the discovery of oil, the global rise in oil prices in the mid-2000s was the point when Dubai really started to imprint their ambitions on the world and their opportunity to make the city a lasting success for centuries to come.

Just 50 years ago, the city was one of lackluster infrastructure with no means or enticement for foreign investment. Fast forward 50 years and not even Sheikh Rashid Al Maktoum could have imagined the success the city has so far achieved.

Of course, the transformation of Dubai wouldn't have been possible had it not been for the discovery of oil but even so, the oil wasn't discovered in eternal quantities. The plan since the discovery has been meticulous with a clear view of how the new found fortune would be invested.

The global oil price increases in the 2000's allowed for the city to invest and focus on speedy development of essential infrastructure.

Today's Dubai

After the construction of the two tallest hotels in the world, the city wasn't to stop there. In 2004, plans were approved for the Burj Khalifa. The building was finished in 2009 and instantly became the tallest building in the world and by some distance, standing at a remarkable 829 meters tall.

The current ruler, Sheikh Mohammed bin Rashid Al Maktoum, came into power in 2006, and is credited with creating the boom within the city in a variety of industries such as real estate, tourism, finance, and more. As a result of his vast efforts to make Dubai a sustainably wealthy city, just five percent of Dubai's current revenue comes from oil.

Know Before You Go

Before we delve into Dubai's different areas, its transportation system and its other particularities, we will first take more of a general look at this unique place.

Visa Requirements

Visa requirements for entering Dubai vary greatly between different nationalities and it is always advised to check regulations before traveling. Information and eligibility may have changed since this guide was written.

Citizens of the following countries (including all 28 EU member states) will get their visa upon arrival at all UAE airports or other points of entry. This includes those who hold visas in their passports or entry stamps from other countries and the visa is valid for 30 days, renewable once. The countries at the time of writing are:

Australia, Austria, Andorra, Belgium, Brunei, Bulgaria, Canada, Cyprus, Croatia, the Czech Republic, Denmark, Estonia, France, Finland, Germany, Greece, Hong Kong, Hungary, Iceland, Ireland, Italy, Japan, Latvia, Liechtenstein, Lithuania, Luxembourg, Malaysia, Malta, Monaco, Netherlands, New Zealand, Norway, Poland, Portugal, Republic of Korea, Romania, San Marino, Singapore, Slovakia, Slovenia, Spain, Switzerland, Sweden, United States of America, United Kingdom with (Right of Abode in UK) and the Vatican.

GCC Nationals
National citizens of GCC countries (Gulf Cooperation Council: Bahrain, Kuwait, Oman, Qatar and Saudi Arabia) do not require a visa to visit the UAE. Visas will also be issued to escorts/domestic helpers of GCC nationals for a renewable duration of 60 days.

GCC Residents who are not GCC nationals but hold high professional status such as company managers, doctors, engineers or employees working in the public sector and their families are eligible for a non-renewable 30-day visa upon arrival at all UAE airports or other points of entry.

The original passport of the sponsored person, valid residency visa and proof of employment in the country of residence is required for visa.

For all other nationalities, a visa must be applied for before the visitor enters the country either through their respective embassy, a local UAE sponsor or a local hotel.

Types of Visas
The Dubai Naturalization & Residency Department (DNRD) issues different types to visas.

Visit Visa
Tourists who wish to stay in UAE for more than 14 days or those coming on family or business visits can apply for Visit Visas. These are valid for either 30 days (short term visit visa) or 90 days (long term visit visa). Both visas are non-renewable. Apart from the visa fees, a deposit is to be paid

by the local sponsor/ relative/resident which is reimbursed after the visit visa holder has left the country.

90-Day Long-Term Visit Visa for individuals is valid for 60 days from the issue date and non-renewable. Valid for 90 days from the arrival date and non-renewable.

30-Day Short-Term Visit Visa for individuals is valid for 60 days from the issue date and non-renewable. Valid for 30 days from the arrival date and non-renewable.

Documents required (Individuals):
• Clear passport copy of the sponsor
• Clear passport copy of the sponsored person
• A copy of the salary certificate or employment contract of the sponsor (resident) must be attached
• Proof of family relationship (kinship)
• Travel insurance

Tourist Visa
The tourist visa is a special category under the visit visa type and entitles the holder to a 30-day stay and is non-renewable.

If the holder of the tourist visa stays for more than 30 days, that person has to pay a fine per day plus some charges for an out pass.

Sponsorship of hotels and tour operators who bring in visitors is required for tourist visa. Individual tourists from Turkey, Ukraine, Albania, Russia, St Kitts-Navis, St Lucia, Mexico, Cuba, Bermuda, Belize, Guyana, French Guiana, Martinique, Antigua and Barbuda, St Vincent, Jamaica, Palao, other non-defined American nationalities, Thailand, South Africa, Singapore, China can apply for this type of visa. A clear passport copy of the sponsor and travel insurance is required for the visa.

Location

Located on the Persian Gulf coast of the UAE, Dubai is a city which is situated just 16 meters above sea level. It stands to the northeast of the UAE and is the second largest emirate in the country.

Dubai shares borders with Abu Dhabi to the south, Sharjah to the northeast and Oman to the southeast. Dubai covers an area of 4,110 km^2, which represents an expansion of 200 km^2 from its original size due to reclaimed land from the sea.

The city also benefits from a unique geographical location which allows for a strong strategic location connecting the city to all of the Gulf States in the area and also to the East of Africa as well as South Asia.

Dubai lies directly in the Arabian Desert. However, the topography of Dubai is vastly different from that of the south of the UAE in that much of Dubai's landscape is highlighted by sandy desert patterns, while gravel deserts dominate much of the southern region of the country. The sand consists mostly of crushed shell and coral and is fine, clean and white.

East of the city, the salt-crusted coastal plains, known as sabkha, give way to a north-south running line of dunes. Farther east, the dunes grow larger and are tinged red with iron oxide.

Climate

Being located in the Arabian desert, it will come as no surprise to hear that Dubai experiences a tropical desert climate with conditions often very hot and sunny, especially in the summer.

The summer months in correlation to the hot conditions can be extremely humid with very dry temperatures tending to reach 40 °C and beyond and very rarely going down past the 30 °C mark.

Dubai is a city where the temperature is warm all year round, even in the winter. The winter months can range from highs of up to 23 °C with lows dropping to approximately 14 °C.

Despite the weather often consisting of warm temperatures, the previous decade or so have seen a gradual increase of rainfall to the city. Despite that, Dubai's rainfall, like all cities in the region, is very brief with the annual rainfall reaching just 150mm in recent times.

A large proportion of Dubai's annual rainfall happens during the winter months between December and March with the climate staying warm.

The months between December and March are well known to be the most comfortable throughout the country with the climate being at a moderate and bearable temperature and perfect for exploring the city by foot without the prospect of experiencing a heat stroke or dehydration.

Statistically, the month of February is the wettest with a rainfall on average of 35mm. June is the driest month in the city with rainfall down to an absolute minimum if nothing at all.

In the summer months, low pressure systems develop over the city which subsequently create strong north-westerly winds known locally as Shamal. They blow over from Saudi Arabia and can often be extremely unpredictable by the time that they reach Dubai. The Shamal often stirs up the desert sands which can vastly reduce visibility and create sandstorms which can last several days.

Because Dubai consists of such different regions, temperatures and humidity can vastly differ between both the coastline and the desert. In the winter months, the climate on the coast is warmer while the climate in the desert is a lot cooler. The humidity is also higher on the coast compared to the dry heat of the desert and the sea can even reach as high as 37 °C with humidity of more than 90%.

Currency

The official currency used in Dubai and the United Arab Emirates is the United Arab Emirates Dirham.

As an official fixed exchange rate, the Dirham is pegged to the U.S. Dollar meaning that 3.67 UAE Dirhams are always equal to 1 U.S. Dollar.

The UAE Dirham has an official abbreviation of AED and is subdivided into 100 fils.

Coin denominations consist of 25 fils, 50 fils and 1 Dirham. Banknote denominations consists of 5, 10, 20, 50, 100, 200, 500 and 1000 Dirhams.

Population and Languages

Dubai today has one of the fastest population growths of any country in the world.

The population as of October 2016 is estimated to be around 2.6 million people. This is even more remarkable considering that 45 years ago in the year of the formation of the UAE, Dubai had a population of just 300,000 people.

The population growth of Dubai during the last decade averages at an astonishing rate of between 5% to 8% per year which makes Dubai one of the fastest growing places in terms of population on earth.

Of course, with the rise of Dubai as such a prominent and important city over the last 30 years and the popularity that it has experienced, it is no surprise to hear that the rise in population growth is mainly down to the vast influx of foreign nationals from all corners of the globe who have come to work and live in the city.

As well as becoming a financial and business hub in that period, the city has equally become a fashionable and sought after tourist destination. The number of tourists visiting the city is a hugely expanding aspect with more than 12 million tourists per year.

The official and most commonly spoken language in Dubai is Arabic. However, with a great number of the population residing in the city coming from foreign lands, it is more than common for English to be spoken by the majority of the population, both in a

out of the professional workplace.

Visitors to the city will have no trouble communicating with locals and getting by in English and most of the road, shop signs and food menus are commonly in both the English and Arabic languages.

Religion

While some neighboring countries adopt for a more conservative and strict following of Islam, the practicing of other religions in Dubai is well respected and allowed.

People with other faiths to Islam are allowed to build houses of worship on privately owned land and invite people of that religion to practice on the premises. In fact, as of 2016 there are currently 33 Christian churches located in the United Arab Emirates.

However, despite allowing for the practice of other religions, it is illegal to preach the ideas and values of any religions other than Islam through media or literature. Those caught are likely to face prosecution and deportation from the country.

Although it is illegal for non-Muslims to preach about their religion, it is perfectly legal for those groups to advertise religious functions in the name of celebrations, gatherings and events in the local media.

Religious holidays such as Christmas, Easter and Diwali are also marketed by a small proportion of businesses who sell items and products for those occasions.

During the Islam holiday of Ramadan which takes place during the ninth month of the year, it is illegal to drink, eat and smoke in public between sunrise and sunset – for both Muslims and non-Muslims, although exceptions are made for pregnant women and children. People who break these very delicate rules will be subject to prosecution by the relevant authorities.

Other religious faiths prominent in Dubai include Christianity, Hinduism and Sikhism. The majority of the Christian minority are made up of Protestants and Roman Catholics. Hinduism and Jainism are both practiced by the majority of Indians and Sindhis who have been living in the country since the early development of the city.

To acknowledge their help in developing the city, the ruler at the time Rashid bin Saeed Al Maktoum allowed for the people to develop and construct a temple complex in the city along with a Sikh temple.

At this time, there are no Jewish synagogues in the whole of the UAE with the very small population of Jews living in Dubai commonly practicing their religion in private.

Tipping

There is no written rule stating that visitors (or expatriates) have to tip for a service, but just like any other tourist haven, it is general agreed that if the service has met expectations then a tip should be given.

If you are happy to tip for the service that you have received, there is no official amount that you need to give but the general consensus is that a tip between 10% and 15% of the final bill is sufficient.

With the rise of services in Dubai to accommodate the needs of tourists, the city has somewhat gained a reputation for being a place with very high standards of customer service. The people giving you that customer service are extremely hard workers and will often go that extra mile to ensure that your experience exceeds all expectations.

Naturally, tipping is not for everyone, with some people expecting quality service to be included in the initial price. Tipping varies from industry to industry and it all falls on personal preference.

Tipping in Dubai is rarely expected and no matter how small the amount, it is always greatly appreciated.

The most common form of tipping comes in the restaurant industry by rewarding your waiter or waitress for their efforts. It shouldn't be forgotten that wait staff in Dubai can often be on low basic salaries with a large proportion of their monthly income deriving from tips. Most restaurants will state at the bottom of their bills that taxes and a service charge have been included in the total price but tipping your waiter or waitress if very common dependant on quality of service.

Taxis are in great abundance around the city and it is very common for visitors to utilize this service to travel from their hotel to the days attraction or whether it is traveling from nightclub to nightclub. Taxi drivers in Dubai are mostly pleasant and extremely knowledgeable and it is common for passengers to tip between 5 and 10 AED for their efforts.

In Dubai, it is also common for people to

tip for beauty services such as a masseuse or hairdressers but once again this all depends on the quality of service. For services such as beauty treatments then it is common for people to give a tip between 10 and 15 percent whereas with a haircut or a massage, the tip is generally bigger.

When visiting the supermarket, customers will be greeted at the check out by some very cheery and energetic bag-packers. These bag-packers generally see hundreds of shoppers each working day so it is common to tip them with small change and a 'thank you'.

When receiving a take away, whether it is some food or a grocery shop, it is common to allow the driver to keep the change as a token of your gratitude.

The Local Culture

Dubai is a unique and vibrant metropolitan city with people from over 100 different nationalities living in harmony. Despite this, the local culture is still very much rooted in Islamic tradition.

Dubai is just like all other countries in the Arab world in that courtesy and hospitality are apparent in abundance while also being a prized virtue. The locals are accepting, friendly and welcome people from all backgrounds, religions and ethnicity to the city with open arms.

Visitors should, therefore, also be accepting of the local culture and laws. The city is a Muslim city and with that, there are many considerations to be taken into account by foreigners visiting the city to avoid causing offense.

Religion:
Mosques of traditional and breathtaking beauty can be found scattered all over the city and the sunset call to prayer can be heard across the rooftops each day. In Dubai, the official weekend starts on Friday and at midday mosques are bombarded with followers meeting to listen to a sermon. The majority of stores in the city will open in the afternoon at 2:00pm after the sermon has finished.

Clothing:
Although there is no official dress code in Dubai, it is widely expected and appreciated for tourists to dress conservatively, especially women. Those who ignore this advice and walk around the streets wearing very little are likely to get strange looks from locals. At the beach, it is accepted for women to wear a bikini and for men to be shirtless and donning just swimming shorts or speedos.

In the streets of Dubai and in shopping malls, men should avoid wearing shorts above the knee and going topless while for women, it is expected to avoid wearing clothing that exposes a large amount of skin such as short skirts, short t-shirts and hot pants. It is advised for women to wear full length t-shirts and blouses.

Women from Arab states commonly wear a full length black robe called an ‘abaya’ - it is regarded as a local custom. Muslim women are required to cover their heads and to wear long clothes covering both their legs and their arms.

Traditional and common clothing for men is a ‘dishdasha’ which is a full length white robe complemented by a white or red headdress

is commonly known as the 'gutra'.

Other Customs:
Of course, tourists love to take photos and there is no better place to create a beautiful picture than in Dubai. However, taking pictures of Muslim women can cause great offence. It is strongly advised to ask for permission before taking a picture of a Muslim women and in most cases, she will politely decline your request.

Tourists should also be aware that some Muslim men and women tend to avoid shaking hands with people of the opposite sex, which is a strong Islamic tradition. Tourists are advised to wait and see if the other person lends their hand first to avoid causing offense. The most common form of greeting for local men is by touching noses or kissing cheeks.

Public displays of affection between members of the opposite sex, both Muslims and non-Muslims are strongly frowned upon and visitors should also avoid kissing or holding hands and keep it in private.

For people not familiar with the Arabian culture, you may be surprised to see local men holding hands - this is a sign of strong friendship.

Hospitality:
If you are lucky enough to be invited into a local's home, remove your shoes before entering, as per tradition. You must also remember to avoid pointing the soles of your feet in anyone's direction, as this is extremely rude in the Arab Muslim culture.

Arab Muslims are known to be extremely hospitable and if invited to their home, then you can expect an awful lot of food and drink to be on offer. When taking something to eat or to drink, you should take it with your right hand with the left being left for things such as using the toilet.

The locals of Dubai are extremely generous and they will make sure that you have eaten more than your fair share and you may even have to decline a few times before they acknowledge that you are in fact full.

Ramadan:
Before visiting Dubai, an essential aspect to learn about is the Islamic religious holiday Ramadan. Failure to learn about the strict rules can often result in severe punishment as well as causing great offence to the local people.

The Holy Month of Ramadan occurs during the ninth month in the Islamic calendar and is observed by Muslims worldwide. The month consists of between 29 – 30 days (based on a visual sighting of the crescent moon) of fasting in order to commemorate the first revelation of the Quran to Muhammad according to traditional beliefs.

Fasting occurs every day during the month from dawn until sunset. During this time, Muslims avoid eating, drinking, smoking and also engaging in sexual contact. Muslims should also refrain from behaviors which could be considered sinful such as insulting others, cursing and lying.

Tourists visiting Dubai during the month of Ramadan are expected to respect the tradition in public places. Both Muslims and non-Muslims by law are not allowed to eat, drink and smoke in public places.

Whereas the majority of restaurants will be closed during the day, more and more eateries have appeared in shopping malls which are fenced off from public view. During Ramadan, these eateries are open during the day for non-Muslims.

Away from the public eye in private such as in a hotel room, these restrictions don't need to be followed and it is acceptable to drink, eat and smoke. Most hotels will keep their restaurants open all day albeit with sectioned off areas, so if you have booked a hotel with half or full board, then you will still be able to utilize your package.

It is also very much expected for visitors to dress conservatively during the month of Ramadan to avoid causing offense. Avoid wearing short skirts and items of clothing which show off too much skin. Visiting Dubai during the month of Ramadan is a fantastic way to experience the Islamic culture and although it can be quiet during the fasting hours, the city truly comes alive after sunset with people everywhere and the atmosphere booming.

Local Laws

Although Dubai is renowned as a modern and tourism based city, it is very much an Islamic city and tourists should be aware on what is permitted and what is not. It is vitally important for visitors from the Western world to realize that laws, standards and expectations they are used to at home may differ to those in Dubai.

The city, although more liberal than some of its neighbors is still a very conservative place and is under Sharia Law. There can be serious consequences if the law is broken. Police statements and legal proceedings are all issued strictly in Arabic, which for non-Arabic speaking westerners can be extremely intimidating and frightening.

It is vitally important to stay on the correct side of the law, and the best way to do that is to be as knowledgeable as possible before your visit. A frightening statistic for visitors is that even a minor offense can lead to a 23-day stay in jail, which is the duration on average for the first hearing in a local court.

As a visitor, you should be made most aware of alcohol, co-habiting and public decency laws, all of which are explained below. Be sure to research any other laws that many apply.

Alcohol Laws
Despite gaining a reputation of being a glamorous party destination over the past decade, being a Islamic country governed by Sharia Law, Dubai has strict alcohol laws.

An overview of alcohol tolerance in Dubai is simple. You are only allowed to drink alcohol in licensed premises. This is restricted to four and five star hotels and the restaurants, bars and nightclubs on the premises. Drinking alcohol is in no way tolerated in the public eye either on the streets or on the beach.

Visitors are also strongly advised that although it is perfectly okay to be drunk in the premises of a licensed establishment, drunken behavior is not tolerated in public places and will instantly land you in prison.

Over the past few years, it has been made possible for non-Muslims to buy alcohol in off-licenses which are located in shopping centers on the outskirts of the city. However, to buy alcohol from these stores, consumers are required to hold an alcohol license.

Alcohol licenses are pretty easy to get hold of and they need to be renewed each year. It is vitally important for people keeping alcohol in their house or even transporting alcohol to hold a license as without it, then it is classed as an illegal offense. Drink driving is forbidden and comes with a hefty punishment.

Public Decency Laws
Although it is perfectly acceptable for couples to show minor public displays of affection such as holding hands, anything beyond that is highly frowned upon and illegal.

Of course, anything behind closed doors in a hotel room is not off limits but while in the public eye, it is strongly advised to be it tasteful and keep affection to the bare minimum.

In Dubai it is a criminal offense to be rude or disrespectful to others. Although in the western world it would seem crazy to be sent to prison for using foul language or pointing your middle finger at somebody, doing such things in Dubai could land you with a 30 day spell in the local prison.

Co-habiting Laws
Strictly speaking, living or sharing a hotel room with a member of the opposite sex to which you are not related or married to is against the law. The punishment for this is often one-year imprisonment, followed by deportation. However, although sharing a hotel with your boyfriend or girlfriend is technically illegal, the police don't go looking for unmarried couples and hotels do not ask you if you are married to the person you are checking into a room with.

Best Time to Visit

Due to the soaring and humid temperatures that Dubai experiences in the summer months, climate wise, the best time to visit the city is between November and March.

Dubai is warm all year round so it really isn't a case of trying to avoid the cold and bad weather, but rather trying to avoid the searing heat.

The winter months are very much the peak months with many tourists clambering to the city. The weather during these months is perfect for adventuring around the city without the humid temperatures.

The temperatures during the winter months range from 20°C (68°F) and 27°C (81°F) which make for the perfect climate to explore this budding city and to walk across the white beaches without being burnt to a crisp and potentially experiencing heatstroke.

This time is generally the busiest period of the year and it is advised to make hotel and excursion reservations a good few months in advance.

It should also be noted that between January and March it tends to be the rain season, but you shouldn't be put off by this as showers are often very brief.

Tourists hoping to avoid the peak season crowds should look to visit the city between April and October. However, although you will have more freedom to just turn up to the main attractions without a reservation, temperatures can reach up to the mid-40s, which can often make it unbearable to be outside.

Getting There

Getting to Dubai is easy - it is extremely well connected by its international airport to most of the world and can be accessed by other means too.

Flights

Dubai International Airport
Ranked as the third busiest airport in the world in terms of passengers, the Dubai International Airport is the primary route of traveling to the city. In 2015, the airport handled 78 million passengers.

Built in 1960, the original airport contained just 6,000 ft of runway, a hanger for a limited number of planes and a small terminal. Five years later in 1965, a new runway, made from asphalt was opened with a length of 9,200 ft which was run next to the original sand made runway. Technological improvements to the airport were also made, with the addition of navigational aids and an extensive lighting system.

At the end of the decade, the airport was serving nine airlines from 20 destinations across the world. The expansion of the airport continued in the 1970s with adjustments made to accommodate bigger and more advanced aircraft.

With Dubai's intentions of becoming a world popular tourism destination, more and more airlines introduced routes to serve the city and the year 2000 saw the completion and official opening of a second terminal known as the Sheikh Rashid Terminal.

With increasing numbers descending onto the city, it was very apparent that the airport would require a third terminal and with construction starting in 2004, the terminal was eventually opened in 2008 after a two year delay and became the world's biggest airport terminal; it expanded the airport's capacity by 47 million passengers per year.

Dubai International Airport, also known as DXP, covers over 7000 acres of land and in 2015 accommodated 403,517 flights coming in and out of the airport. DXB is situated in the east of Dubai, 4.6 kilometers from the city center. The airport is the hub for international airline Qantas, Flydubai and Dubai's flag carrier Emirates.

Emirates has the exclusive use of Terminal 3. 65% off all passengers who travel through DXB are handled by Emirates.

As of late 2016, there are 8,000 weekly flights to and from the airport operated by over 140 different airlines to 270 destinations, including direct flights to and from most large capital cities.

One of the biggest draws of DXB is the duty free. Dubai Duty Free (DDF) is the largest single airport retailer in the world. On the anniversary of the airport's opening, Dubai Duty Free slash the prices of a wide range of its products. The promotion normally runs from the 18th December until the 20th with the discount in 2015 being 25%.

Taxis are located outside of all the terminals and are in abundance with the twenty to thirty minute journey to the city centre typically costing 60 to 80 AED. Between 8:00pm and 6:00am, there is a 25 AED night surcharge. There are also taxi's specifically for women located outside of all terminals.

The Dubai Metro is also another fast and affordable option to reach the airport. Trains run from terminals 1 and 3 at intervals of approximately every 10 minutes. Services start at 5:30am and stop at midnight (1:00am on Friday morning). On Friday the service starts at 1:00pm. Fares at 3 to 7 AED per person one-way, depending on the distance travelled.

Local buses are also available, though you need a Nol pre-paid smartcard to use these as buses do not take cash. We recommend taking the metro instead. A Sky bus operates directly from many hotels to all terminals at the airport - pricing is 15 AED (twice the price of metro).

Al Maktoum International Airport
The Al Maktoum International Airport, also commonly known as Dubai World Central opened in 2010 and is located in Jebel Ali 37 kilometers south-west of Dubai. When the airport first opened, it was only for cargo flights and as of today, the airport is predominantly used for cargo flights with just a handful of airlines operating from the airport that include Wizz Air, Azerbaijan Airlines, flydubai, Finn Air, Qatar Airways and Thomson Airways.

With the airport handling just under 500,000 passengers in 2015, a mere speck of the passengers that fly into Dubai International Airport, Dubai World Central is very much still in the first phase of a long term plan. The whole project was expected to be implemented by 2017, but due to the recent global financial crisis, the completion date has been put back until 2027.

On arrival to the airport, passengers will be greeted with a whole host of taxi's and shuttle buses. The one hour taxi journey from Al Maktoum Airport to Dubai city center will typically cost 140 AED.

The F55 bus is the only bus that runs during the day from the airport with the final destination being Ibn Battuta metro station. The journey takes roughly 45 minutes to Ibn Battuta and from here there are numerous other connections to get to your destination. The route runs from 6:00am until 10:00pm and leaves the airport on the hour.

The night bus (F55) runs to Satwa bus station via Ibn Battuta between 10:00pm and 6:00am and leaves on the hour. The airport is facilitated with duty free shopping, prayer rooms and wifi.

Sharjah International Airport
Due to its proximity of only 15km from Dubai central, Sharjah International Airport has continued to see a rapidly increasing number of passengers each year as Dubai International airport struggles to satisfy demand.

Air Arabia are the principal carrier of the airport but other airlines such as Air India, Egypt Air, Pakistan International Airways, Qatar Airways and Uzbekistan Airways also service the airport. The airport has experienced a rapid rise over the last 5 years, with almost 12 million passengers passing through the airport in 2015 as opposed to 6 million in 2010.

There are two options in order to reach Dubai from Sharjah airport with both taxi' and a shuttle bus by Air Arabia in constant operation. Passengers should be aware that although the distance between Dubai and the airport is just 15 kilometers, the traffic between Sharjah and Dubai is often chaotic and it can take up to two hours during rush hour. The cost of a taxi between Sharjah Airport and central Dubai can range from 50 to 80 AED.

Abu Dhabi International Airport
Many visitors to Dubai choose to fly in and out of nearby Abu Dhabi International Airport.

Featuring three passenger terminals and serving over 20 million passengers per year, the airport is the second biggest in the UAE after Dubai International Airport. The airport is also one of the only in the world that offers flights that fly non-stop to all of the continents. The airport is the hub for Etihad Airways which is the second biggest airline in the UAE after Emirates.

A large and modern airport, Abu Dhabi International Airport offers all of the facilities expected from such an internationally renowned airport. A vast and wide range of duty free stores are available in addition to internet access, executive lounges, a business center, prayer rooms, financial services and showers.

Taxis located outside each of the three terminals are available in their hordes and a journey from Abu Dhabi International Airport to Dubai City Center should take around 1 hour and 10 minutes depending on traffic. The price will typically be around 200 AED for the journey.

Buses

The entire UAE and Oman are well serviced with frequent buses running to and from Dubai. Buses are owned and run by the government of Dubai and are branded under the name Emirates Express. They provide comfortable and air conditioned buses from Dubai city to each of the six capital cities of the Emirates that make up the UAE.

The most popular route is run to Abu Dhabi, the capital city of the country. Buses to the capital, which run every 40 minutes, start from early morning each day and take up to 2 hours depending on traffic. Buses to Abu Dhabi can be taken from both Ghubaiba Bus Station (bus no. E100) and Ibn Battuta Metro Station (bus no. E101) arriving into Abu Dhabi's main bus station. The cost of a one way fare in either direction is 25 AED.

For tourists looking to make the most of their UAE adventure and wanting to visit the less known emirate of Sharjah, then there are several buses running each day from Dubai. Services start from various stations including Gold Souq, Al Karama, Baniyas Square, Jebel Ali and also Al Ittihad Square and commence at Sharjah Jubail Bus Station. As of 2016, the price of a one way fare is 10 AED with the journey taking roughly 45 minutes.

Buses operate from Dubai to Al Ain every hour from the Al Ghubaiba Bus Station in Dubai. Al Ain, also known as The Garden City due to its breathtaking greenery, is the fourth largest city in the UAE and travelers won't be disappointed. The journey takes roughly two hours. Alternatively, tourists wanting to travel to Al Ain can take an Al Ghazal mini-bus from Al Ghubaiba Bus Station and Bur Dubai Taxi Station and take around 1 hour and 45 minutes at a cost of 20 AED one way.

The emirate of Fujairah from Dubai takes the longest out of any of the Emirates but it is a journey that won't disappoint. The bus can take up to four hours and leaves from both the Rashidiya Metro Station and Union Metro Station at a cost of 25 AED one way.

International routes bus routes are also in operation run Dubai to Muscat, Oman four times daily with Al Khanjry Transport. The company provide an efficient journey in modern buses. Buses leave Deira City Center Metro Station at 3:00am, 3:30am, 6:00am and 7:00am. Depending on stops and searches at customs, travel time can sometimes can take up to five hours on the weekday and up to six at the weekend. Passengers are advised to arrive at the place of departure at least 30 minutes before. Tickets can be purchased online from the Al Khanjry Transport website or from the ticket office next to Caravan Restaurant close to Deira City Center Metro Station.

Transportation

Now that you have arrived in Dubai, it is time to look at your transportation options for getting around. Due to innovation in recent years, Dubai has both a modern public transportation system and a great road network.

Public Transport

With over 12 million visitors visiting Dubai each year, a efficient and modern transportation system is a necessity.

Transport facilities have boomed in recent times and Dubai currently has one of the most extensive and advanced transport networks in the world for a city of its size. The transport system in Dubai allows for residents and visitors to get around the vast and vibrant city quickly and comfortably.

There are a vast amount of options to travel around the city with public and private services including Metro, Taxi, Public Bus, Private Bus, Monorail, Trams, Boats, Ferries and luxury vehicles.

Tourists who want to make the most of public transportation in Dubai will need to purchase a Nol travel card. The cards are prepaid smart cards which can be used on all forms of public transport including the bus, water bus and the metro. Nol cards come in four different types (gold, silver, red and blue) and can be reloaded for further travel.

All cards can be reloaded with travel credit to avoid the hassle of buying a new Nol card for each trip, except the Red card which comes in the form of a paper ticket at a price of 2 AED.

The Red cards are only valid for up to 90 days or ten trips and are ideal for short term visitors to the city. A Red Nol card can be purchased from ticket machines located in metro and bus stations with the fare to be pre-paid with the correct journey type before travel.

For the tourists visiting Dubai for over one week, or for those who wish to exploit the extensive public transport network at a rapid rate, then it is recommended to purchase the Silver Nol

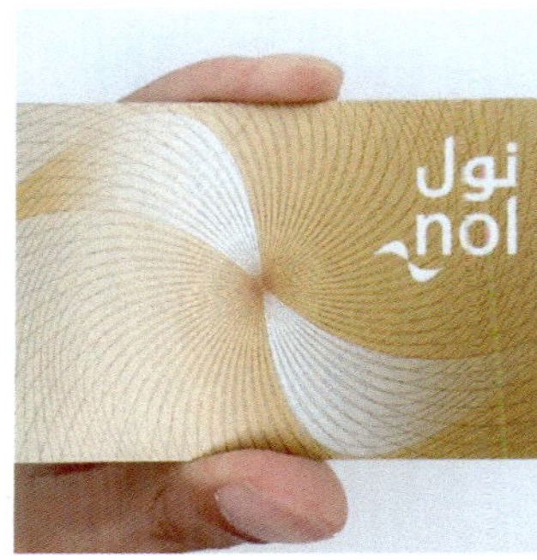

card. This card can be purchased for a price of 20 AED (includes 14 AED of credit) and unlike the Red card is valid for up to five years. The card also has an e-purse meaning that the fare is automatically deducted from your balance after your journey.

There are a number of ways and options in which to buy and reload a Nol card, with the most popular option being to buy the card in the metro station or bus station before travel. You can also buy the cards from RTA customer service centers and official sales agents located in most shopping malls, convenience stores and supermarkets.

When you buy a Gold or Blue Nol card for the first time, proof of identity (either a passport or driving license) will be required upon purchase. Children under the age of 5 or below 90cm in height are permitted to travel on the network for free.

Using a Nol card is extremely simple and they are used In the same fashion as most big city metro, tram and bus networks. Before walking through a turnstile, simply place the card on to the reader and wait for a beep. When the beep is heard it means that you have enough pre loaded funds on the card to travel. When exiting the station of your destination, be sure to once again touch your card on to the reader when you walk out of the turnstile. Please note that if you forget to touch your card when exiting, then you will be charged a maximum fee of 14 AED for the day.

Your Nol card is charged at the end of the journey; the cost is calculated depending on the number of zones passed. Fares for a single journey within one zone start from 3 AED.

Taxi

With over 8,000 taxis serving the city, taking a cab is by far the easiest way of getting around the city. Taxis are in abundance on every corner of the city.

You can hail a cab or use one of the taxi ranks situated around the city. Ranks are mostly outside shopping malls and large hotels.

The taxi drivers serving the city are combined from both government operated companies and also private ones.

The public operated taxi's are run by The Dubai Transport Corporation and they can easily be identified by their cream color.

With government run taxis, to save money, hail a taxi from the street as the starting fare will be just 5 AED instead of the 12 AED starting fare when booked from the taxi firms control center between 6:00am and 10:00pm. After 10:00pm, there is an night surcharge of 10%.

The rate per kilometer is 2 AED and the minimum fare is 10 AED. When taking a taxi from the International Airport the starting rate is 20 AED. It is company policy that if a taxi meter isn't running, then the fare will be free.

For women travelling without a man, there is a women-only service operating within the city; they can easily be identified by their cream and pink colored roofs. This service is also operated by the DTC.

For DTC taxis you can pay with cash, credit card or your Nol Card balance (a small surcharge applies for non-cash payments).

To book a DTC taxi from the control center, call +971 042080808.

There are also plenty of private taxi companies. Private taxis are roughly the same price as the DTC run ones. Please note the final fare can usually only be settled with cash for non-DTC taxis. The most popular companies are: Emirates Taxi: +97143394455; Metro Taxi: +97142673222; and National Taxi: +97143390002.

Metro

Still a relatively new method of transport in Dubai, the construction of the brand new metro system started in 2005 with the red line opening September 2009. The red line was extended in both 2010 and 2013 and as of 2016 there are 29 stations along the line running from Rashidiya to Jebel Ali.

The second line, the green line, began opened in 2011 and today it currently has 20 stations running across it running from Etisalat to Creek. The total length of the whole metro system is 75 km, of which 13 km is underground. Due to the rapid and continuing popularity and expansion of the city, the Dubai government plans to further extend the metro network with a further three lines in the future.

When using public transport and the Metro in Dubai, visitors should be vary of causing offense and the possibility of being issued an on the spot fine by the transport police and security personnel. Eating, drinking, smoking and leaving rubbish are strictly prohibited on public service and if caught will result in an instant fine. This includes drinking water and chewing gum.

People who are drunk are prohibited from traveling on public transport, and transporting alcohol is also not allowed. Animals traveling on public transportation are also not allowed. However, guide or service dogs for those with disabilities are an exception to the rule.

There are also special women and children -only carriages that men may not enter.

Tram

The most recent method of transport to be constructed is the tram network, which opened in late 2014.

The current tram network consists of 10.6km of route with 11 trams servicing 11 stations in total. The planned second phase, which has commenced construction will add an extra 4km of route, an additional 14 trams and 8 stations.

The Tram service currently runs between Mall of The Emirates and Dubai Marina and runs along the busy Al Sufouh Road and Jumeirah Beach Road.

On average, there is a tram every 6 minutes with trams running for 19 hours per day from 06:30 until 1:30. Please note that on Friday, Tram services begin at 09:00 and run into until 01:30.

As of 2016, there has been no official time guidelines given by the government in regards to when the second phase of the

tram network will begin construction.

Passengers wanting to travel via the Tram network will be required to use a Nol card which can be purchased from any metro station and official sale agent.

Monorail

One of the most impressive transport features in Dubai is without doubt the Palm Jumeirah Monorail. The monorail was opened in 2009 and as of 2016 is the only monorail in the whole of the Middle East.

The monorail is located on the Palm Jumeirah Island, Dubai's first artificial island, and connects it to the mainland. The monorail network consists of one line and four stations, although two stations are currently not in operation.

The route is three miles long and runs between Gateway Station located in Al Sufouh and the Atlantis Aquaventure Station where the Atlantis Hotel and Aquaventure waterpark are situated.

Future plans for the opening of Trump Tower Station and Palm Mall Station are planned for the near future.

Although there is no direct connection between the Monorail and the Metro, there is a link between Gateway Station and the Palm Jumeirah Tram Station via a footbridge. You can then connect to the Metro network via Dubai Marina Tram Station and Jumeirah Lakes Towers Tram Station.

The walk from the monorail to the nearest Metro Station takes roughly 10-15 minutes.

Due to the Monorail transport system being owned by a private company, the use of Nol cards is not permitted to travel via the Monorail. A one way ticket costs 15 AED with a return journey costing 25 AED.

Children under the age of five travel for free. The Monorail is in operation for 12 hours per day from 10:00am until 10:00pm, and trains depart on average every 20 minutes.

Bus

Dubai has a vast and extensive bus network and is a vital cog to the city's advanced transport system. Run by the government owned RTA, as of 2016, the bus network consists of 193 routes during the weekdays and transports over 30 million people to and from their destinations per week.

There are more than 600 bus stops in the city with the majority of those having air conditioned bus shelters.

All buses are modern and are air conditioned which is a savior, especially in the summer heat.

There are various types of bus routes including express journeys, feeder bus routes, Intercity bus routes, local bus routes and also CBD bus routes. The size of the bus depends on the type of route taken.

Due to the demand of people reliant on using bus services on a daily basis, buses are often severely overcrowded, especially during rush hour.

In crowded areas, it is usual for people to have to wait up to an hour just to get inside of the bus. For visitors traveling to the city, it is advised to avoid taking the bus from central areas during busy periods as it will make for a frustrating experience, especially when taxis are available and very much affordable.

As is the case for using all forms of public transport, to travel on the bus passengers will require a Nol card which can be purchased from all bus and metro stations, and also official sale agents located in most shopping malls, supermarkets and convenience stores.

For more information on bus routes, please visit the RTA website at www.rta.ae - click "English" on the top left.

Water Travel

One of the most scenic and relaxing ways to get from A to B in Dubai is water travel. The various watercraft are often cheap and a fantastic way to see Dubai's most famous landmarks from a sea view. In fact, traveling by water, either by taxi or bus is one of the oldest methods of transport in Dubai.

In a city which is dominated by beautiful coastline, there are several methods of water transport available to the public and they are often utilized by both residents and tourists looking to experience a new way of being transported from one side of the city to the other.

Abra

An Abra is a traditional part of the Dubai landscape and their existence is in abundance. Manually rowed boats with asphalt pitched side layers, taking an Abra is a great way to experience local traditions while seeing some incredible scenery along the way.

Rich in heritage and charm, Abras are available to take for the majority of day and night and a ride usually costs slightly more than 1 AED.

The Abra sticks to one route between Deira and Bur Dubai and takes roughly six minutes in total. There are two types of Abra available: the traditional version from the Public Library Station and Creek Park Station, and also a rowing abra which are available throughout Dubai Creek and travel to Deira and Bur Dubai.

For tourists who wish to spend a little bit more time in an Abra to take in the sights, then an electrical Abra is available which acts as a tour boat. The electrical Abra is considered to be a luxurious experience that tours Burj Lake while also performing impressive on-board shows. An electrical Abra boat tour can be taken for a price of 60 AED for 30 minutes.

Water Taxi

For tourists who wish to experience a more luxurious ride across the waters of Dubai and experience a level of great comfort and privacy, then a water taxi should be considered. Water taxis can be booked to the nearest station and are able to offer much more flexibility than an Abra - these travel all over Dubai Creek.

Water taxis are in operation from morning until night and can be booked simply by calling +97-8009090. To rent a water taxi for one hour will cost you 400 AED but you can travel to as many different places in that hour as you wish.

For set routes, one stop will cost 50 AED to your desired stop.

Water Bus
An alternative way to travel the waters of Dubai is by a water bus. Run by the government owned RTA, the water bus provides a comfortable experience with air conditioned boats allowing for a smooth and stress free ride across Dubai Creek.

The boats are equipped with comfortable seats and sufficient space while also being available for a very reasonable price. The cost for a one way ticket is 2 AED with payment made with a Nol card. For passengers with special needs, each station is fully equipped with service officials to assist passengers in embarking and disembarking the boat. Travel time from Dubai Creek to Dubai Marina is roughly 15 minutes.

Driving in Dubai

For tourists visiting Dubai, it isn't recommended to rent a car and drive yourself.

Although it is perfectly legal for tourists to rent a car with a valid international driving license, the traffic congestion can mean that it is unlikely to be a pleasant experience driving around the city, especially without prior knowledge and familiarity with the roads and system.

Dubai experiences the most congestion in the whole of the Middle East and commuters spend two hours on average going to and from their place of work.

Although the government has invested greatly to the infrastructure of the roads, the expanding population of the city means that the infrastructure is far behind keeping up with the number of vehicles.

With the option of a number of different methods of transport in Dubai, and with much of it being relatively cheap, it is strongly advised for tourists to avoid the experience of driving on the roads of Dubai and to simply stick with traditional and public modes of transport.

However, for those who are determined to master the roads of Dubai, there are a number of internationally renowned rental companies including Sixt Rent-A-Car and Thrifty Car Rental, as well as local rental companies.

Despite the current problems with the Dubai traffic system and congestion, the government is working hard to improve the situation and commutes for residents and have stated their intentions to construct a further 500 km of roads by 2020.

Neighbourhood Guides

Dubai's different areas - or neighborhoods - all have aspects that make they unique. In this section, we cover them all. Dubai's neighbourhoods have been broken down into the following in this guide:

- Jumeirah
- Palm Jumeirah
- Deira
- Downtown Dubai
- Bur Dubai
- Dubai Marina
- Jebel Ali
- Further Afield

As we look through each neighborhood, we have included a brief description and history of the area, a look at accommodation options, along with popular attractions and places to eat. Organizing the guide in this manner allows you to find a neighborhood you like, and then find local places to visit, stay and dine.

Each attraction, restaurant and accommodation listed features a fact sheet with symbols, the key below helps to explain what each of these symbols means.

Nearest metro station	Website
Opening Hours	د.إ Entry price in AED
Address	Phone number

Jumeirah

One of the most exclusive and affluent districts in Dubai, Jumeirah (often called the Beverly Hills of the Middle East), is a haven for wealthy expatriates residing in the city.

The rise of the area began in the 1990s with the rapid expansion of housing developments across the city. The area instantly became one of the most affluent areas and popular with expatriates due to its location. The area is located close to the coast while retaining a relatively central location.

These days, Jumeirah is extremely sought after and house prices can sometimes reach into millions of US dollars.

Jumeirah is popular with tourists due to the many attractions here including the Jumeirah Beach Park, Jumeirah Mosque and the Wild Wadi Waterpark.

As well as top attractions, there is a wide range of exclusive and high class dining opportunities in the area ranging from local cuisine to international restaurants.

The biggest and most recognizable attraction in the area is without doubt the Burj Al Arab hotel, the third tallest hotel in the world. Tourists flock to the area to get photographs of this impressive piece of architecture.

Attractions

Mercato Shopping Mall

Al Ghubaiba	Free
+971 4 344 4161	10:00 to 22:00 Sunday to Wednesday, 10:00 to 00:00 Thursday to Saturday
Jumeirah Beach Rd	www.mercatoshoppingmall.com

The Mercato Shopping Mall is a medium-sized shopping mall and one of the biggest shopping malls located in Jumeirah. The architecture of the building is a unique design influenced by the Italian Renaissance.

There are many attractions located within the mall including over 150 stores, a cinema, a family entertainment center, banking options, bars, and restaurants located on the first floor.

Food establishments located on the first floor food court include Pizza Hut, KFC, McDonalds, Subway as well as Chinese, French and Italian food. Starbucks Coffee and Costa Coffee are also located here.

Cinema facilities are run by Vox Cinemas and contains 7 screens showing the latest movies.

The family entertainment center is called Fun City packed

with video games, a play area, a ball pit and a climbing frame for children.

Stores situated in the mall include Laura Ashley, Next, Virgin Megastore, Areej and various other outlets dealing in jewelry and watches, lingerie, cosmetics and children stores. One of the biggest draws to the center is Spinneys, which is one of the largest supermarket chains in Dubai.

The Mercato Shopping Mall is a great way to spend a few hours when in the area, with many visiting to take pictures of the wonderful architecture.

Jumeirah Beach

Jumeirah Lake Towers or Dubai Marina

Free for public beach. Jumeirah Beach Park costs 5 AED

Jumeirah Beach

+971 4 348 0000 (hotel)

Saturday to Wednesday 7:30 to 22:00, Thursday & Friday 7:00 to 23:00

One of the top attractions and must-do activities in Jumeirah is visiting and basking in the glorious Jumeirah Beach.

Filled with some of the world's whitest sand, tourists flock to the beach in their hordes to relax in the year-round sun while admiring the views of the Burj Al Arab and the Jumeirah Beach Hotel along with various other skyscrapers that overlook the beach.

The beach stretches 26.4 kilometers along the district of Jumeirah from Jumeirah Beach Residence to Jebel Ali. Some sections of the beach are private and others are public.

Water temperatures in the winter months are 22°C (71°F) whereas in the summer months the water can reach up to 34°C (93°F).

The most popular time of the year to visit the beach is during the winter months where the climate is often a very bearable temperature.

Jumeirah Mosque

Al Jafiliya Metro Station, cross the bridge and then take the X28 bus	د.إ 20 AED
Saturday until Thursday at 10:00. No reservation required.	+971 4 353 6666
Jumeirah Beach Road	www.visitdubai.com/en/pois/jumeirah-mosque

A spectacular piece of architecture to grace Jumeirah is the beautiful Jumeirah Mosque. One of the most recognizable landmarks in Dubai, the mosque was constructed using just white stone as to medieval tradition.

The mosque is large enough to hold over 1,000 worshippers at any one time and it is one of the only mosques in the Middle East and the only one in Dubai that welcomes non-Muslims to enter to take a guided tour.

Tours of the Mosque are available for non-Muslim tourists six days per week and will allow visitors to gain a thorough insight into Islamic culture and the values that it teaches.

The guided tour lasts 75 minutes.

The mosque is lit up at night which allows for tourists to gain a different view of the remarkable beauty that it possesses.

When entering the Mosque, women are kindly asked to wear a head scarf to avoid causing offense.

Wild Wadi Water Park

Al Jafiliya Station, cross bridge & take the X28 bus

د.إ 275 AED for persons above 1.1m tall & 230 AED for persons under 1.1m

10:00 to 18:00 daily

+971 4 348 4444

Jumeirah Road, next to Jumeirah Beach Hotel

www.jumeirah.com/en/hotels-resorts/dubai/wild-wadi/

The Wild Wadi Water Park is a located in Jumeirah between the Burj Al Arab and the Jumeirah Beach Hotel and features three pools and a total of 17 water slides.

Originally opened in 1998, the water park was redesigned and improved in 2008 to meet growing demand from tourists to the city.

The current design of the water park is unique in the sense that it is the first aquapark in the world to link chains of the rides together, meaning that visitors can enter rides without actually having to leave the water. Unlike other aqua parks where you have to leave the water in order to join the queue for a ride, the Master Blaster takes visitors to the top of the rides in the water.

The most popular rides in the park include the White Water Wadi and the Riptide FlowRiders surfing experience.

Other popular features of the park include the six downhill ring rides and the Jumeirah Sceirah, which is the tallest and fastest free fall waterslide outside of North America with speeds reaching up to 80 kilometers per hour.

Other facilities to feature at the water park include private and spacious changing rooms, chill out shaded areas and a whole range of food and beverage opportunities.

Dubai Zoo

Al Jafiliya Station, + X28 Bus + 8 min walk

د.إ 2 AED

10:00 to 18:00 daily. Closed Tuesday.

+971 4 349 6444

Jumeirah Street

Visiting Dubai Zoo is a fantastic and cheap way to spend a few hours while in Jumeirah.

Dubai Zoo is one of the oldest icons of the emirate and was built in 1967 with the patronage of the then ruler of Dubai, Sheikh Rashid. He gave the go-ahead to the construction of the zoo and it became the first zoo to be built in the Arabian Peninsula.

The zoo is located on Jumeirah Street close to the Jumeirah Shopping Center and Mercato Center, and at present the zoo in maintained by the Dubai Municipality.

When the zoo opened for the public, it did not house many animals. The limited collection included a few big cats, monkeys, and other mammals, and to house a few reptiles and fish, there was a small aquarium. From 1986 onwards, the zoo was greatly expanded.

The zoo currently hosts about 230 species of wildlife. The animal population comprises of big cats like Lions, Jaguars, Pumas, and other wild animals like Hyenas, Foxes, Chimpanzees, Monkeys, Giraffes, Deer, and Porcupines, to name but a few.

There are about 1,000 individual animals, which includes endangered species like the Bengal tiger, Siberian tiger, Arabian wolf, Arabian wildcat, grey wolf, and gorilla.

In the birds section, you will find ostriches, parrots, and golden eagles, while there are other close to 400 reptiles as well.

This site is expected to close in early 2017 with the animals being relocated to the huge new Dubai Safari Park.

Dubai Aquarium and Underwater Zoo

- Burj Khalifa/Dubai Mall
- +971 4 448 5200
- The Dubai Mall, Doha Street
- د.إ 100 AED
- 10am-11pm (Sun-Weds) and 10am-12pm (Thurs-Sat)
- www.thedubaiaquarium.com

Located in the Dubai Mall, the Dubai Aquarium and Underwater Zoo is a breathtaking and truly spectacular visitor attraction in the Jumeirah area and is always full of tourists wanting to experience a modern aquarium.

The aquarium has the capacity to hold up to 10 million liters of water and offers 270-degree views throughout the 48-meter long aquarium tunnel.

The prominent feature of the aquarium is the main water tank which measures at 51 meters by 11 meters and is 20 meters deep.

Visitors flocking to the attraction will also be able to enjoy the underwater zoo which houses a vast range of marine species and is located on the second floor. Other displays include penguins, crocodiles, piranhas, lizards, snakes and otters.

Shoppers in the Dubai Mall can enjoy views of the tank for free directly from the middle of the shopping center. The tank is extremely impressive, and houses over 30,000 aquatic animals including a vast variety of sharks and rays.

Although seeing and viewing such aquatic animals is more than satisfying for most, for those who wish to get closer to the action, then additional experiences like glass-bottomed boat rides, cage snorkeling, shark dives and PADI speciality dives are available.

The entrance to the Dubai Aquarium and Underwater Zoo is located on the Ground Level of the Dubai Mall.

Dining

Flooka
Address: *Dubai Marine Beach Resort and Spa, Jumeirah Road*
Opening Hours: *12:00 to 15:30 and 19:00 to 0:00.*
Phone: *+971 4 346 1111*
Website: *www.flooka.com*

Located in the Dubai Marine Beach Resort and Spa, this specialist luxury seafood restaurant describes itself as a unique dining experience of the best in Mediterranean seafood with a Lebanese twist. Visitors dining at the restaurant will be able to enjoy views of the beautiful Arabian Gulf from the terrace.

As well as enjoying a seafood feast, diners can also exploit the full bar, outside terrace, Wi-Fi and shisha facilities.

A meal for two will cost about 300 AED.

Loca
Address: *Dubai Marine Beach Resort and Spa, Jumeirah Road*
Opening Hours: *12:00 noon to 02:00.*
Phone: *+971 4 346 1111*
Website: *www.locauae.com*

Loca, which can be found in the Dubai Marine Beach Resort and Spa, is a modern and popular Mexican bar and restaurant.

Opened in 2009, Loca offers a different kind of Mexican experience usually found outside of Mexico. Unlike the usual fast-food aura attached to Mexican food, Loca has produced an experience for people to really enjoy the luxury of an authentic dish in a unique ambience.

In the years after opening, Loca has become one of the trendiest places in Jumeirah welcoming a vibrant international crowd. Loca is the perfect place to come with friends, family or even with work colleagues to enjoy a relaxed atmosphere with premium food and drinks, live sport and live music.

A meal for two including an alcohol beverage will typically cost in the region of 400 AED.

Turkish Village Dubai
Address: *Jumeirah Beach Road*
Opening Hours: *07:00 to midnight*
Phone: *+971 4 344 9955*
Website: *www.turkishvillagedubai.com*

Turkish Village Dubai Restaurant and Cafe is a popular restaurant offering Turkish cuisine. The restaurant offers a unique and rich carnival of the senses that gladdens the heart, delights the eye and captivates the soul. The interior of the restaurant is very much influenced by Turkish culture and allows visitors tto experience an enchanting Turkish atmosphere.

The menu has great variety with main dishes served with a heap of aromatic rice, grilled tomatoes, peppers and onions. Also on the menu are succulent wraps and sandwiches, as well as fresh and delicious salads, which are perfect for lunch after a serving of the fragrant lentil soup.

The outdoor dining area and terraces are a wonderful place to meet and dine and provide the perfect backdrop to any evening.

A meal for two will generally cost 200 AED.

Kabana Restaurant and Cafe
Address: *Villa #517, Jumeirah Beach Road*
Opening Hours: *12:00 noon to 03:00. Closed Wednesday.*
Phone: *+971 4 388 1111*
Website: *www. kabanarestaurant.com*

Situated in the heart of Jumeirah, Kabana Restaurant and Cafe is a luxury eatery offering some of the best Afghan and Mediterranean cuisine in the Middle East.

The restaurant, although small, offers a contemporary twist to the finest traditional dishes, offering diners exquisite grilled delights and an impeccably relaxed ambience. Diners are encouraged to enjoy total relaxation by indulging in the unique and truly delicious flavors of the authentic cuisine.

Kabana offers a vibrant atmosphere and is very popular with locals, although tourists are very much welcomed and catered for with the utmost professionalism.

The terrace is the perfect place for guests to unwind and lounge while enjoying a tasty mocktail or smoothie. Other than the delicious food on offer, other facilities provided include a shisha area and live musicians.

A meal for two will typically cost 220 AED.

Hotels

Burj Al Arab
Address: *Jumeirah Beach Road*
Phone: *+971 4 301 7777*
Website: *www.jumeirah.com/Burj-Al-Arab*

Arguably the most famous and recognizable hotel in the whole world, the seven-star Burj Al Arab is both a leading tourist attraction in Dubai as well as being the hotel everybody wants to stay in – but only the wealthiest can afford.

Currently the third tallest hotel in the world at 280 meters tall, the Burj Al Arab's most prominent feature is the location where it stands. Built on a man-made island, it is only possible to reach the hotel by passing on a private bridge which is heavily manned by security.

From the local public Jumeirah Beach, tourists gather to take and share pictures of this breathtaking piece of sail-shaped architecture. The hotel is the ultimate symbol of the city's luxury, innovation and wealth.

All of the suites in the Burj Al Arab, as suggested from the exterior are all super-luxurious. With panoramic views of the sea and the Dubai Skyline, flat screen TV with hundreds of channels, Bose speakers, a media hub, iMac, gold plated iPads and impeccable and spectacular furniture and decor, the Burj Al Arab really has it all.

The resort features two large outdoor swimming pools for guests to relax, a helicopter transfer service, a world class concierge service, an oversized and luxurious spa center with infinity pool, hot tubs and saunas, a fitness center, tennis courts, squash courts, luxury cabanas, a business center and dry cleaning services.

In addition to the world class facilities located on the premises, there is also nine world class signature restaurants overseen by some of the

most famous chefs in the world.

There is also a wide range of bars with different themes and atmospheres for guests to enjoy a vibrant evening with friends and family. The most popular bar located on-site is The Sky View Bar which allows for guests to enjoy the ultimate view suspended 200 meters above sea level.

Beach Hotel Apartments
Address: *Jumeirah Beach Road*
Phone: *+971 4 345 2444*
Website: *www.beachhotelapartment.ae*

Located in the heart of Jumeirah next to the Grand Mosque, Beach Hotel Apartments offer modern and luxurious apartments equipped with top of the range furniture and decor.

The apartments are serviced daily and two-bedroom apartments are also available to rent. The location of the apartments means that it is just a five minute walk to the white sands of Jumeirah Beach. A wide range of restaurants and cafes are also located close by for easy access from the apartments.

Each apartment comes with internet access and various communal facilities including a temperature controlled roof top swimming pool with sea views.

The apartments also include the use of a fully equipped gymnasium, secure basement parking and 24-hour serviced front desk. The Turkish influenced decorated apartments include a flat-screen TV, DVD player, a fully equipped kitchen and also a dining room.

Holiday Inn Express Jumeirah
Address: *Jumeirah Road*
Phone: +971 4 407 1777
Website: www.hiexpress.com/Jumeirah

Holiday Inn Express Dubai Jumeirah is a budget two-star and comfortable hotel in Dubai located next to landmarks such as Jumeirah Mosque and Dubai Creek.

The 193 rooms at the Holiday Inn Express are all well decorated and modern and are all equipped with air conditioning.

Other room facilities include a coffee/tea maker, a safe, direct-dial phone, fax machine, iron and ironing boards, a desk and a hairdryer. As well as those facilities, each room features a TV with premium and satellite television channels.

Guests wishing to connect to the internet can do so with the internet access provided in the room. The reception is open for 24 hours per day.

The hotel restaurant is open from early morning until the late evening from where guests can enjoy a wide range of different dishes from countries all over the world. The hotel prides itself on their friendly and courteous members of staff with the vast majority able to speak a variety of different languages.

Additional services provided by the hotel include child care, dry cleaning/laundry service. The business center located at the hotel provides conference and meeting rooms.

Palm Jumeirah

Palm Jumeirah is the largest man-made island in the world. The artificial archipelago is shaped as a Palm tree featuring 17 fronds and a surrounding crescent.

After years of construction, the Palm Jumeirah finally opened in 2006 and instantly became synonymous with the city.

Today, the island is home to thousands of people in modern and luxurious homes while it is also a prominent attraction in the city of Dubai.

On completion, the island added an incredible 320 miles of shoreline to the city.

The project is just one of three planned by the city and when the other two are finished, all three artificial islands will be known as the Palm Islands.

The Palm Jumeirah is so vast in size, that it can be seen from space.

Attractions

Aquaventure Waterpark

Palm Atlantis Monorail

د.إ 260 AED

+971 4 426 0000

10:00 to 17:30 daily

Atlantis, Crescent Road, The Palm Jumeirah

www.atlantisthepalm.com/marine-water-park/aquaventure-waterpark

The Aquaventure Waterpark is regarded as not only the best waterpark in Dubai, but also in the Middle East and is on the premises of the renowned Atlantis Hotel.

Located to the north of the artificial Palm Jumeirah island, the waterpark will be sure to give you the thrill of a lifetime.

Not only does the waterpark feature some of the most adrenaline pumping rides in the world including The Tower of Neptune and The Tower of Poseidon, but it also features a whole host of experiences to make the your day at the Aquaventure Waterpark one that you will never forget.

For an additional charge, guests to the park can experience a whole host of activities such as getting up close and personal to sharks and rays and riding the Atlantean Flyer Zipline.

Guests can of course enjoy relaxing on the 700 meters of Aquaventure coastline.

Dining

West 14th Steakhouse
Address: *Oceana Beach Club, Palm Jumeirah*
Opening Hours: *12:00 to 15:00 and 19:00 to 23:00*
Phone: *+971 4 447 7601*
Website: *www.west14th.ae*

West 14th Steakhouse is one of the most renowned and exclusive restaurants on the Palm Jumeirah. With its American theme, regular live music and spacious terrace, West 14th Steakhouse is one of the places to be.

In the winter months, when the weather is more mild, the restaurant really is at its peak. The impressive terrace is full of elaborate diners overlooking the water and observing the Dubai Marina skyline.

The whole experience is as rich as the price of a meal and diners will be relaxed by the resident band who play an array of chilled out music to really set the tone.

The food is delicious and succulent with some of the finest cuts of steak in the whole city. It is a real high class steak eating experience that comes with a whole host of fine touches.

See the accommodation section below for some more restaurant recommendations inside Atlantis.

Accommodation

Atlantis, The Palm
Address: *Crescent Road*
Phone: *+971 4 426 2000*
Website: *www.atlantisthepalm.com*

Situated on the iconic Jumeirah Palm Island, the Atlantis hotel has become synonymous with the man-made artificial 'eighth wonder of the world'.

Arguably the most recognizable hotel in Dubai after Burj Al Arab, visitors flock to the site of the hotel in order to enjoy and take pictures of the breathtaking and expansive architecture.

Guests staying at the hotel will be able to enjoy the private white sand beach in addition to taking advantage of the great view of the Arabian Gulf.

Facilities provided by the hotel are of the very highest quality including an underwater aquarium, a water park, tennis courts, squash courts, a fitness center and a children's club.

The rooms are warm and spacious and are influenced by the local Arabian culture. Every room has a balcony with a scenic view, a seating area, flat screen TV, minibar and a large bathroom with an oversized spa.

Guests staying at Atlantis will also be able to exploit a range of award winning restaurants that are located at the resort.

The most famous of them all is Yuan which delivers the finest Chinese food. Other award winning options include Nobu, which offers Japanese cuisine and Bread Street Kitchen whose menu was personally created by Gordon Ramsay. In addition to a variety of restaurants, there is also a range of bars and nightclubs present on the premises.

Deira

Located in the north-east of the city of Dubai, Deira represents one of the first established commercial and financial areas to appear in the city and today is still an important commercial and residential district.

The Deira district also represents the more traditional side of modern day Dubai with a wide range of Souks dealing in spices, gold and perfumes.

The vast majority of Souk owners are able to speak English and for those visitors hoping to experience some real UAE culture, then this a great place to come in order to fulfill those needs.

Souk vendors are not just salesmen, and they are often happy to elaborate on old traditional stories.

Located just north of Dubai Creek, people visiting the area often come directly after visiting the impressive Creek.

This more authentic side of this area is a great reason to visit Deira and escape the hustle and bustle of Downtown Dubai and Jumeirah.

Attractions

City Center Deira Shopping Mall

Deira City Center	Free
+971 4 295 1010	Saturday to Wednesday from 10:00 to 22:00, closing at 0:00 on Thursday & Friday.
8th Street, Dubai	www.citycentredeira.com

Located in the heart of Deira, the shopping center features over one million square feet of space consisting of retail stores, restaurants, cinemas and private services.

The mall features close to 400 stores ranging from fashion outlets, cosmetics, children's toys, electronic goods and art with the highlights being Carrefour, Debenhams, Paris Gallery, Virgin Megastores, Zara, H&M and Hollister.

Located on the third floor, the food court offers over 60 outlets, both domestic and internationally influenced.

The mall also features a range of entertainment facilities including VOX Cinema City which offers 11 screens showing the latest movies.

Bowling City is a popular haunt amongst families and offer a cosmic bowling experience as well as a children's arcade, karaoke and billiards.

Magic City is an entertainment center which is also popular amongst families as facilities include simulators and video games, ideal for children.

Dubai Creek

Dubai Creek is the most prominent historical point of the city and is something that visitors to Dubai simply must explore and experience.

The Dubai Creek has always been critical to Dubai's success; it was the location where trade with foreign lands began over 100 years ago.

Separating the Bur Dubai area of the city from Deira, one of the most popular tourist attractions on the creek is to take a traditional Abra water taxi or bus and cruise from one side to the other.

A ride on an Abra is beautiful and allows you to see the more historical and original side of Dubai.

Whether you opt to take an Abra across the creek or simply decide to take a picnic and just relax on the banks located next to it, the experience of Dubai Creek will be a cultural and inspirational one.

A renowned aspect of the city, there are many restaurants and hotels located along the banks of the creek to allow tourists the chance to really soak up the relaxing atmosphere that it gives to the city.

Al Ahmadiya School and Heritage House

Al Ras

د.إ Free

+971 (0)4 226 0286

Saturday to Thursday 8:00 to 19:30, and Fridays from 14:30 to 19:30

Al Khor Street

www.visitdubai.com/en/pois/al-ahmadiya-school-and-heritage-house

One of the must do and see attractions in the Deira area of Dubai is without a doubt visiting the heralded Al Ahmadiya School and Heritage House. Featuring breathtaking architecture, visitors of all backgrounds who visit this 100 year old school can gain a great insight of the culture of the city.

Founded in 1912 by a well off Pearl merchant, the school was very unique when it was formed as it featured two floors and was attended to by the children of wealthy pearl merchants who made their fortunes from the boom of the industry during this time.

After ceasing operations as a place of education, the school was renovated and reinvigorated into a museum, primarily to show the history of traditional education in the emirate.

The museum contains many interesting artefacts including virtual technology of its history.

The museum gives visitors a great insight into Dubai's rich past through the decor, furniture and artefacts on display in the building.

Deira Clocktower

Deira City Center | Al Maktoum Road

The Deira Clocktower, also known as the Dubai Clocktower, was built in 1963 and then restored in 1973. It is situated before the Maktoum bridge on a roundabout and is one of the area's most recognizable landmarks.

The story behind the construction of the Clocktower is certainly an interesting one with it originally being a gift from a wealthy Sheikh to the ruler at the time, Sheikh Rashid, in order to celebrate the first oil export from the country.

It was an exciting time in the country and the gift was designed to be a lasting monument that represents a time when Dubai became financially viable to expansion.

The clock tower took approximately 10 months to complete and was designed by a Syrian national called Zaki Al-Homsi who was specifically sought out to build the impressive feature.

In fact, Sheikh Rashid was so impressed by the final results that he offered Zaki Al-Homsi UAE citizenship which he duly accepted.

Voted in 17th place of the most beautiful clock towers in the world, the Deira Clock tower, with all of its history and significance is certainly a must see monument and one that won't cost a single dirham to see.

Gold Souk

Metro	Al Ras	Price (د.إ)	Free
Address	54 Al Khor Street	Hours	Saturday to Thursday 10:00 to 22:00, Friday 16:00 to 22:00

One of the must-do things when visiting Deira and Dubai is to explore the old traditional Gold Souk.

Traditionally known as a place to pick up a bargain and purchase cheap gold, walking through the breathtaking Gold Souk is an essential. Not only will you be able to experience conventional Dubai culture and traditions, but you also might pick up some beautiful accessories, even if you're not prepared.

The Gold Souk is the most genuine place to pick up gold in the city and those wanting to make a purchase can be rest assured that your piece of gold will be genuine and high quality. One of the beauties of buying gold here is that the price advertised is not the price that you will necessarily have to pay.

Salesmen and women shifting gold are always open to haggling customers and in some cases, if you play your cards right and show some charm, you will be able to get up to 30% off the original asking price.

Be persistent and show your authority by walking away if they won't give in and nine times out of ten they will call you back and accept your final price.

There are hundreds of vendors operating in the souk offering a whole range of jewelry including Gold, Silver, Diamonds and also other types of stones and metals. Prices tend to be according to the current trading price with the addition of a few Dirhams.

Dubai Creek Golf and Yacht Club

Deira City Center	From 265 AED per person
+971 4 295 6000	See website as these change often.
Baniyas Road, Port Saeed	www.dubaigolf.com/dubai-creek-golf-yacht-club

Golf enthusiasts visiting the Deira area are very well catered for.

Opened in 1993, the Dubai Creek Golf and Yacht Club is one of the most affluent and beautiful golf clubs not just in Dubai, but in the whole of the Middle East.

Located beside the creek, the 18-hole championship course is a pleasant and rewarding experience with beautiful scenery and testing obstacles.

Also housing one of the first golf schools in the UAE, the sail-shaped clubhouse comprises function rooms, conference rooms and fine dining facilities to enjoy after a round.

For those less interested in golf, and more fascinated with the yacht part of the name, the yacht club is located adjacent to the golf clubhouse and marina and houses a number of restaurants, function rooms and also a board work.

The site is also home to the Park Hyatt Hotel to accommodate visitors who wish to relax in the green and chilled out surroundings for more than just one round of golf.

Dhow Wharfage

Deira City Center	د.إ Free	Baniyas Road

To catch an insight into Dubai's trading and maritime history, then there is no better place to visit than the Dhow Wharfage.

Although modern day Dubai is popular with visitors wanting to make the most of white sandy beaches, the impressive cuisine and the lavish lifestyle the city has to offer, visitors wanting to complete their trip with an intake of culture and history of the city need not look any further than the Dhow Wharfage.

Situated in the Deira area of Dubai amidst the Deira Old Souk and Al Sabkha station, Dhow Wharfage offers visitors a unique insight into the old traditions of Dubai which have been immaculately kept in order despite the vast evolution the city has experienced of the last few decades.

Located in the wharfage are impressive Dhows (boats) which have been constructed from wood and have been maintained 100 years later. It is an incredible sight to see an old Dhow unloading cargo of a whole range of products from flat screen TV's to tubs of tobacco.

Emblazoned with the flag of The United Arab Emirates, the Dhows' normal delivery route is to neighboring countries around the Arabian Gulf.

For tourists who long for a dose of UAE tradition and culture, then visiting the Dhow Wharfage is a must-do. Even for tourists not necessarily looking for a dose of history, visiting the Wharfage is an admirable and extremely interesting way to spend an hour or so.

In some cases, tourists who take a significant interest in the tradition have been known to be invited on board to listen to tales of the crew's experiences over a cup of coffee.

Mamzar Beach Park

Mamzar Beach Park Terminal (Bus/Coach)

Car entrance - 30 AED + 5 AED per person, Pool - 10 AED adults, kids 5 AED

+9714 2966201

08:00 to 22:00 daily

Mamzar Beach Park is a beautiful 260-acre plot of land that offers locals and tourists alike a whole host of facilities.

The area is especially perfect for families as the park offers picnic areas, 28 barbeque areas, a children's play area, roller skating, volleyball, sport areas, restaurants and even bicycle rental to fully explore all that the park has to offer.

The highlights of the park certainly include the five private beaches that feature some of the whitest sand in the world.

If swimming in the sea doesn't excite you, then there are always the three swimming pools on offer, all equipped with changing areas, showers and on duty lifeguards.

For visitors wanting to spend the whole day at the park with added comfort and for a place to retreat, you will be pleased to know that the park has air conditioned chalet's for rental which are equipped with private barbeque areas and showers.

One of the biggest draws to the park is the impressive amphi-theater. Located in the center of the park, it is often home to music concerts for you to enjoy.

Dining

Legends
Nearest Station: *Deira City Center*
Address: *Deira, Port Saeed*
Opening Hours: *12:00 to 15:00 and 19:00 to 23:00.*
Phone: *+971 4 295 6000*
Website: *www.dubaigolf.com/dubai-creek-golf-yacht-club/indulge/legends*

Legends is a mid-range steakhouse restaurant located in the beautiful scenery of the Dubai Creek Golf and Yacht Club. Specializing in meat, visitors to the restaurant will be in awe of the perfectly cooked steak and relaxing ambience while overlooking the beautiful green and impressive Dubai Creek. The restaurant decor features an abundance of long glass windows so diners can enjoy the beautiful scenery inside of the building as well as on the specially designed terrace.

The highlights of the menu include the Australian Lamb Rack, the Calves Liver, The Legends Burger and the Pan Fried Fillet of Sea Bass.

The busiest time at the restaurant is the famous Friday Brunch in which live music with a Jazz duo and a DJ are available between 12:00 and 15:30 to set a vibrant tone. Set menus for the Friday Brunch include an unlimited starter and dessert buffet in addition to your order from the a la carte menu.

Legends Steakhouse also hosts a monthly wine tasting evening. Included in the set price is a four-course meal with a different glass of wine to complement each course with a wine expert delivering background information.

Guests planning to eat at Legends should be aware that the dress code is smart casual.

Al Dawaar Revolving Restaurant
Nearest Station: *Deira City Center*
Address: *Al Khaleej Rd*
Opening Hours: *12:30 to 15:30 and 18:30 to 0:00.*
Phone: *+971 4 317 2221*
Website: *www.dubai.regency.hyatt.com/en/hotel/dining/AlDawaar*

Specializing in Arabic, Japanese and Mediterranean cuisine, the Al Dawaar Revolving Restaurant is the only revolving restaurant in Dubai offering diners remarkable views of the city, the coast and also the impressive Dubai Creek.

With a relaxed and sophisticated aura, this is a great place to enjoy great company, succulent and rich food and also spectacular views of the city.

Highlights of the vast menu include the Veal Stew with Pumpkin Dumpling and Cumin Seed, the Grilled Lemon with Saffron Lemon, the Blue Crab with Sweet Chili Sauce and also the Hamour Kebab with Chermoula Sauce.

One of the popular highlights of the week is the Champagne Brunch event on Friday which includes an international buffet with a vast mixture of foods and desserts. The Friday brunch runs from 12:00 to 16:00 and the set price per person is 275 AED, which includes unlimited sparkling wine, beers and soft drinks. The dress code is smart casual.

JW's Steakhouse
Nearest Station: *Deira City Center*
Address: *JW Marriott Dubai, Abu Baker Al Siddique Road*
Opening Hours: *Friday to Wednesday from 17:00 to 0:00, Thursday from 12:00 to 0:00.*
Phone: *+971 4 607 7009*
Website: *www. marriottdiningatjw.ae*

One of the most lavish and exclusive restaurants in Dubai, JW's Steakhouse offers not only some of the most succulent steak in the Middle East but also offers an extremely inviting and relaxing atmosphere.

The decor is warm, consisting of a lot of lavish wood with carefully chosen pictures adorning the walls as well as the impressive bull horns. The grand interior also includes a tank which is full of expensive and high quality seafood.

As well as having a reputation of offering some of the finest cooked meats in the city, the restaurant prides itself on the whole dining experience starting from being greeted at the entrance to offering expert advice on food, wines and beers. The staff are knowledgeable and are at your call for your whole experience.

The typical price for two people is roughly 600 AED.

Yum!
Nearest Station: *Union Square*
Address: *Level 1, Radisson Blu Hotel Dubai Deira Creek*
Opening Hours: *12:00 to 23:30*
Phone: *+971 4 205 7033*
Website: *www. radissonblu.com/en/ hotel-dubaideiracreek/ restaurants*

For visitors on a budget but with a desire to eat great food at an internationally renowned eatery, then "Yum!" is for you. Located in the five-star Radisson Blu Hotel, the restaurant specializes in pan-Asian cuisine including Thai and Indonesian food with a vast and expansive menu.

Staff are friendly and knowledgeable and tend to be native to Thailand or Indonesia but with excellent English speaking skills.

Highlights of the menu include the rich in flavor Noodles, the Burmese Chicken Noodles with Laksa and also the impressive Tofu Salad.

The restaurant is fairly informal so there is no dress code and a two course meal with a drink will typically cost 100 AED per person.

Hotels

Radisson Blu Deira Creek
Nearest Station: *Union*
Address: *Baniyas Road*
Phone: *+971 4 222 7171*
Website: *www.radissonblu.com/en/hotel-dubaideiracreek*

Built in 1975, the four-star Radisson Blu Deira Creek hotel is one of the original and first exclusive hotels to open in Dubai and is located in a glorious location in Deira Creek with close links to the International Airport, Jumeirah, Bur Dubai and also Downtown Dubai. The hotel houses 275 rooms of high quality and exclusive furnishings and decor.

Facilities include: nine dining venues offering a wide range of local and international cuisines, a fully equipped fitness center with a gym, tennis courts and sauna and also a business center featuring meeting rooms and conference rooms with the ability to hold over 1,000 people.

For those looking to enjoy an alcohol beverage, a short walk down to the top floor will open up a few opportunities to enjoy the bars on-site with live music and spectacular views of the local area.

The room facilities include private balcony, bathrobes and slippers, high-speed internet access, complimentary coffee and tea, local and international newspapers and also 24-hour room service.

Avari Dubai Hotel
Nearest Station: *Al Rigga*
Address: *Al Rigga Street*
Phone: *+971 4 295 6666*
Website: *www.avari.com/property/avari-dubai*

The impressive four-star hotel Avari Dubai is situated in the heart of the vibrant Deira district and located next to the Clock Tower, one of the biggest and most impressive attractions to the area. Also located close is the vibrant and busy Al Rigga Street.

Dining opportunities include the Olive Tree restaurant which offers an all day international buffet, and also a cafe bar situated next to the hotel reception.

The hotel is also home to a fitness center with a gym and a sauna.

Live music can be found in a few of the on-site night venues and those who wish to party are able to make the most of the on-site nightclub.

Rooms are modern with comfortable furnishings and include a flat screen TV with satellite channels, free internet access, coffee and tea making facilities, a private telephone, air conditioning, a desk, mini-bar, ironing facilities, safety deposit box, hairdryer, 24 hour room service and wake up services.

Pacific Hotel
Nearest Station: *Union*
Address: *Opposite Sabakha Bus Station, Sabakha Street 115*
Phone: *+971-4-2276700*
Website: *www.pacifichotel-dubai.com*

The Pacific Hotel s a two-star budget hotel with basic but comfortable facilities.

The main selling point of the hotel is its location, being close to a range of attractions and monuments such as Deira Clock Tower, Dubai Creek, Deira City Shopping Center, Al Mamzar Beach Park, the Dubai Gold and Spice Souks. It is also just a 20 minute drive from Dubai International Airport.

The hotel features restaurant facilities with a daily international buffet breakfast, in addition to lunch and dinner.

The 32 rooms are basic but clean and include all the facilities you would expect.

Downtown Dubai

Downtown Dubai is right in the center of what is now called 'New Dubai' and is a haven for tourists and wealthy residents. The previous two decades have seen a surge in real estate developments in the area which has resulted into a population of over 100,000 people living in the area, with that number rising significantly each year.

Downtown Dubai is a continuously growing development complex with a wide range of attractions and luxurious hotels enticing people to the area. On completion of the development, it is estimated that the area covering Downtown Dubai will cover over 2km^2.

The main attraction to the area is the Burj Khalifa, which is the tallest building in the world and the crown jewel of Downtown Dubai.

Downtown Dubai also has the world's tallest performing fountain and the world's largest shopping mall, the Dubai Mall and also the world's biggest suspended aquarium.

Downtown Dubai is one of the most impressive districts of the city. Everywhere you go in the area, you will be looking upwards to admire the incredible feat of tall skyscrapers that adorn the city and thinking to yourself just how the city has evolved in such a short space of time.

The Downtown Dubai complex is primarily located along Sheikh Zayed Road and bordered by the Al Wasl district to the northwest, Business Bay to the south and to the northeast by Financial Center Road.

To visit the area by Metro you will need Burj Khalifa/Dubai Mall Station.

Alternatively, visitors wanting to take a stroll to the area can be guided by spotting the Burj Khalifa building, which as the tallest building in the world is a very prominent sight from most areas of the city.

Attractions

Burj Khalifa

Metro	Burj Khalifa	د.إ	At The Top: 200 AED, SKY Lounge: 500 AED
Phone	+971 4 366 1655	Hours	Daily from 08:30 to 23:00
Address	1 Sheikh Mohammed bin Rashid Blvd	Web	www.burjkhalifa.ae

By far the most prominent landmark in Downtown Dubai is the remarkable Burj Khalifa, the world's tallest building. Construction began in 2004 and it opened in 2010 at a cost of more than $1.5 billion. Upon its official opening, the building instantly became the tallest building in the world standing at 829.8 meters. The record dwarfed the previous record of 509 meters held by the Taipei World Financial Center.

The Burj Khalifa was named after Khalifa bin Zayed AL Nahyan, the president of the UAE, and also the ruler of neighboring city Abu Dhabi in recognition for lending the city of Dubai money in order to pay off outstanding debts.

Visitors can purchase tickets to 'At The Top', located on the 124th floor of the building. From here, you will be able to experience 360-degree views. It is a breathtaking experience with unique views of the Arabian Gulf and the city of Dubai. 'At The Top' offers interactive media, high powered telescopes, experts, a gift shop and also a ride in one of the world's fastest elevators.

The highest point of the Burj Khalifa open to the public is on the 148th floor at the Burj Khalifa SKY Lounge. It is just like 'At The Top' but with a lot more luxury and comfort, and it lies 24 floors above the regular experience. Guests will have access to the world's highest outdoor observatory deck which makes for a spectacular experience.

Also located within the Burj Khalifa is the luxury Armani Hotel and numerous restaurants.

Dubai Fountain

Burj Khalifa	Free
N/A	See description.
Downtown Dubai, Dubai	www.thedubaimall.com/en/entertain-detail/the-dubai-fountain-1

The Dubai Fountain, which is located in the heart of Downtown Dubai adjacent to the Burj Khalifa, is the world's biggest choreographed fountain with a repertoire of over 30 different performances.

The fountain is situated in the Burj Khalifa lake and opened to the public in 2009.

It is a large attraction in the area with many people gathering to admire the spectacular show.

The fountain consists of almost 7,000 lights, features 25 projections and comes in at 275 meters in length.

Without a doubt one of the most see attractions in Downtown Dubai, visitors won't be disappointed at the range of prowess and flexibility that the fountain possesses.

The show schedule is as follows: Afternoon shows, daily (except Fridays) at 13:0 and 13:30. Afternoon shows (Fridays only) at 13:30 and 14:00. Evening shows, daily from 18:00 to 23:00, every 30 minutes.

Dubai Mall

Metro	Burj Khalifa/Dubai Mall	Price	Free
Phone	+971 800 382246255	Hours	10:00 to 00:00 Sunday to Wednesday and 10:00 to 01:00 Thursday to Saturday
Address	Financial Center Road, Dubai	Website	www.thedubaimall.com

Dubai Mall is a shoppers' paradise. Staying in line with Downtown Dubai's passion for everything big, this is the biggest shopping mall in the world with an area of over 500,000m^2.

The mall contains roughly 650 retailers and over 1200 stores offering a variety of different goods, products and services.

In addition to being the world's biggest shopping mall by area, Dubai Mall is also the most visited shopping destination with close to 90 million people visiting the mall in 2015. As well as featuring roughly 1200 stores of which all of the world's leading brands are represented, the mall is also an attractive prospect for residents and tourists due to the scale of other facilities on offer on the premises.

One of the biggest attractions to the mall is the impressive Dubai Aquarium and Underwater Zoo, the main tank of which can be seen by shoppers in the mall. The aquarium has a wide many different aquatic animals on display and the Underwater Zoo houses many rare aquatic animals.

One of the prominent leisure facilities is the Dubai Ice Rink. The rink is a fantastic family activity and is also very popular among teenagers. Equipped with music and a light show, the ice rink is the perfect opportunity to perfect and improve your skating ability.

The ice rink is also a multi-purpose venue and can be transformed into a hall with the ability to hold over 2000 people. Dubai Ice Rink is also home to several professionals who offer skating lessons and advanced classes.

The SEGA Republic indoor theme park is a children's and teenagers' heaven featuring over 150 video games mostly with the influence of Sonic The Hedgehog, as well as 15 indoor rides, an amusement arcade, laser quest, bumper cars and simulators.

Movie lovers are also well catered for. Reel Cinemas is a modern cinematic experience featuring an incredible 22 screens and four platinum suites for the ultimate comfort.

After a hard day of walking around the world's biggest shopping mall and attempting to choose between the 1200 stores on offer, visitors to the mall can indulge in a wide variety of different food and cafe outlets located in the extensive food courts scattered around the premises.

There are over 150 food outlets operating in Dubai Mall with a diverse selection of cuisines to choose from to cater to the needs of every individual. Options include fine dining, al fresco dining, international fast food outlets and a wide selection of different themed cafes.

Dubai Opera

Burj Khalifa	د.إ Varies by show
+971 4 440 8888	Varies by show
Downtown Dubai, Dubai	www.dubaiopera.com

Opened in 2016 and located in the opera district of Downtown Dubai, Dubai Opera features impressive architecture and is the location of performances from some of the most renowned opera singers and performers in the world.

In addition to primarily being used as an opera hall, the venue is the first multi-purpose performing Arts Center in Dubai with the design having the ability to be turned into a theatre, a concert hall, a business venue and an exhibition space.

With a capacity of 2000 people, it is one of the biggest dedicated opera theatres in the Middle East.

The design of the building is in the shape of a classic dhow, a traditional sailing vessel still operating out of the Dubai Creek today.

Dining

Wafi Gourmet
Nearest Station: *Burj Khalifa*
Address: *Dubai Mall*
Opening Hours: *10:00 to 02:00am*
Website: *www.wafigourmet.com*

Wafi gourmet is a fine dining restaurant that specializes in authentic Lebanese cuisine. Being located in Dubai Mall, Wafi Gourmet is perfectly situated for shoppers to enjoy some mouth watering and succulent Lebanese influenced dishes after a day of shopping.

Staff are friendly and knowledgeable and they will ensure that your dining experience exceeds expectations and leaves a lasting impression. The warm ambience and traditional decor creates a sublime dining experience.

The menu is vast with highlights including a selection of succulent kebabs, shawarma and also the fresh and locally sourced seafood. For those who have doubts about Lebanese cuisine, the menu also offers a range of perfectly prepared continental dishes. To finish, diners are recommended to exploit the quality homemade ice cream.

A meal for two will typically cost 300 AED.

Social House
Nearest Station: *Burj Khalifa*
Address: *Dubai Mall*
Opening Hours: *09:00 to 0:00.*
Phone: *+971 4 339 8640*
Website: *www.thedubaimall.com/en/dine/dining_restaurants/social-house*

Located on the ground floor in Dubai Mall, the Social House is a unique and eclectic restaurant experience where they believe that eating a meal should be a social activity. Therefore, the layout of the tables is cramped and the majority of tables are eight-seaters. It might not be to everyone's taste, but the close conditions create a bustling atmosphere and have strangers striking up conversation in no time at all – especially after a few glasses of the premium wine on offer.

The menu is extensive, so even the fussiest of eaters will have no trouble finding something. The menu contains a mixture of international dishes such as gourmet pizzas, sushi, British style fish and chips, Malay curries and pasta dishes.

There is an impressive terrace area overlooking the Dubai Fountain and Burj Khalifa, but be sure to make a reservation in advance to secure a table outside. Recommendations from the menu include the lamb shank with red curry sauce, lemon sauce and garlic potatoes, the wok-fried spicy chicken with twice cooked crispy lemongrass and also the Social House lasagne with beef ragout, turkey ham, boiled egg and beef salami.

A relatively affordable restaurant, a meal for two here will cost approximately 150 AED.

Hotels

Armani Hotel, Dubai
Nearest Station: *Burj Khalifa*
Address: *Burj Khalifa*
Phone: *+971 4 888 3888*
Website:
www.armanihotels.com

Branded after world renowned fashion icon Giorgio Armani, the Armani Hotel is one of the most exclusive and luxurious hotels in Dubai. The hotel very much matches the elegant standards and reputation set and enjoyed by the Armani fashion brand.

The only hotel located within the premises of the Burj Khalifa, the Armani Hotel offers the very best of everything. The hotel is spread over 11 floors of the Burj Khalifa and also enjoys a private entrance.

The rooms are spacious, exclusive and elegant with views across Downtown Dubai. The rooms are decorated and the bed sheets are extremely high quality. Facilities included in the room are a large flat screen TV with satellite channels, a DVD player, an iPod docking station, air conditioning, high speed internet, towels, soaps, room service, safety deposit box and a range of international newspapers.

Reception services include 24 hour front desk, currency exchange, excursion organization, luggage storage and a concierge service.

Other prominent features of the hotel include a spa and wellness center, a fitness center, hot tubs, dry cleaning service, shoeshine and ironing services and a gift shop.

The hotel is also home to a range of fine-dining restaurants, a bar and a busy nightclub. In addition, there is a business center for all business requirements.

Al Murooj Rotana, Dubai
Nearest Station: *Burj Khalifa*
Address: *Al Safa Street*
Phone: *+971 4 321 1111*
Website:
www.rotana.com

The five-star Al Murooj Rotana hotel is located in the heart of Downtown Dubai in an impressive grand building of rich architecture.

First impressions of the hotel will certainly be great, and it will only get better once you step inside. The hotel is within walking distance to the Burj Khalifa and the Dubai Mall.

Surrounded by impeccably maintained gardens, one of the hotel's most prominent features is its large outdoor swimming pool - perfect for cooling off after a hard day of exploring the city.

One of the most popular parts of the hotel is the award winning English-style Double Decker Pub which serves the best alcoholic beverages from around the world. The Pergolas restaurant will be sure to whet your appetite and is open all day and offers international dishes. Located in the hotel lobby is the Circle and City café which is a perfect start to the day.

The rooms are luxurious with extraordinary views of Dubai and the pristine courtyard and pool.

Other facilities include a fitness center with a gym and tennis courts, sauna, a steam room and a jacuzzi. Also present on-site is a hair and beauty salon.

Bur Dubai

When visiting Dubai, one of the things that instantly strikes you is how developed and classy everything seems. There are sport cars driving the streets, skyscrapers everywhere, the very latest technologies and people with visual class.

Once you are in the heart of the city and look around, it is sometimes difficult to remember that you are in fact in the desert.

However, some visitors want to seek evidence of the culture and tradition in Dubai. For those people, the Bur Dubai area is a must.

Situated between the Jumeirah district and the Dubai Creek, Bur Dubai is the historical side of modern day Dubai. Tourists flock to the area in their hordes to take in the remarkable mosques and historical buildings standing in the area.

Some of the most impressive pieces of architecture are the Grand Mosque and the blue tiled Iranian Mosque.

In addition to the historical buildings, Bur Dubai is a great place to go shopping. With many Souks in the area and many shopping streets filled with local vendors, the district is a great way to pick up a cheap but authentic souvenir.

Attractions

Meena Bazaar

Al Fahidi | Daily from 10:00 to 22:00

Meena Bazaar is a popular and busy shopping area located in the heart of Bur Dubai. The area is full of stores which offer traditional Emirati products and souvenirs.

The area is also a great place for tourists to find a bargain in the hordes of jewelry stores scattered around.

In some cases, diamond and gold pieces of jewelry can be purchased for up to half the price of what it would cost in a traditional shopping district.

The area is often busy but it is a must visit to experience the local Dubai culture while taking in the unique smells wafting from the many restaurants and street side food stalls.

Bastakia Quarter

Al Fahidi | -971 800 900 | Al Hamriya, Bur Dubai

For visitors that really want to get a true sense of the history and culture of Dubai, then the Bastakia quarter is a must see.

Originally constructed in the 18th century, the village became home to wealthy Persian merchants and then local Arab tribes and the village expanded in the centuries to follow.

It was only upon the discovery of oil in the region, that people started to move out of the village in order to seek a more modern and fancy way of living.

The most prominent features of the Bastakia Quarter are the long narrow streets and the traditional wind towers. The wind towers are especially special in this area as they are great examples of traditional Persian architecture.

Rather outrageously, half of the village was destroyed in the 1970s in order to make room for an office development. There were also plans for the village to be destroyed fully, but after a campaign was started to preserve the area, the plans changed and eventually plans were put in place to restore the original features.

A truly breathtaking and special place, the Bastakia Quarter today is home to a range of attractions such as art galleries, a Heritage House, cafés and boutique hotels while the popular Dubai Museum is located in the area.

For the tourists who want to further their understanding of the history of Dubai, then they should also visit the Sheikh Mohammed Centre for Cultural Understanding where experts will teach you about the customs and traditions of the city.

The center operates walking tours through the Quarter on a daily basis at 9:00am and 10:30am, except on Fridays.

Creekside Park

Metro	Dubai Healthcare City Metro Station 1	Price	AED 5 per person to enter park, Cable Car: AED 25 for adults and AED 10 for kids
Phone	+971 4 336 7633	Hours	08:00 to 22:00 Sunday to Wednesday and 08:00 to 23:00 Thursday to Saturday
Address	Umm Hurair 2, Dubai	Website	N/A

One of the best, most modern and peaceful parks in Dubai, the Creekside Park is the perfect place for married couples, friends and families to hang out and enjoy some nature, greenery and a tranquil atmosphere.

Located on the edge of the Dubai Creek, the park provides the perfect combination of free space with the beauty overlooking the Creek.

The park is a true piece of beauty and certainly one of the most popular and well known parks in the city. Covering a large amount of lawn and botanical gardens, the park really has something for everybody. In addition to being a great place to relax with a picnic, it also provides facilities to keep visitors well entertained.

One of the biggest highlights is the Cable Car. Riding on the only park Cable Car in Dubai allows for visitors to enjoy a bird's-eye view of the park and the surrounding Bur Dubai and Deira areas.

Whether you want to talk a walk along the promenade gazing at the Creek, hire a bike, have a barbeque at any one of the dedicated barbeque areas, or play mini-golf, Creekside Park really has it all. There is even a cactus garden!

The park is also extremely family friendly with plenty to keep the children entertained. There are numerous children's playground scattered around and even a go-kart track to ensure children will be more than content.

Dubai Dolphinarium

	Dubai Healthcare City Center	د.إ	Shows are 120 AED per adult and 70 AED per child.
	+971 4 336 9773		See description.
	Creek Park, Umm Hurair 2		www.dubaidolphinarium.ae

The popular Dubai Dolphinarium was opened in 2008 and has since gone on to achieve unprecedented popularity, especially among families. The Dolphinarium is located in the popular Creekside Park.

The venue is fully air conditioned and offers numerous facilities such as a restaurant, children's entertainment and a gift shop.

Although the Dolphinarium is primarily designed to offer entertainment to spectators, there are also a number of classes and learning facilities to allow guests to learn about dolphins and seals and about their behaviors.

The Dolphinarium is a great way to spend a few hours and you will be entertained and the kids in awe.

The Dolphinarium is open every day between Monday and Saturday with the first show starting at 11:00 and another one at 18:00. On Fridays and Saturdays, there is an extra show which starts at 15:00.

The shows last approximately 45 minutes and will have you smiling from head to toe watching the incredibly friendly and intelligent Black Sea bottlenose dolphins.

In addition to watching a show, guests also have the opportunity to actually swim with a dolphin. To exploit this opportunity, reservations are required in advance.

Dubai Museum

Al Fahidi

+971 600 560000

Al Fahidi Fort, Al Fahidi Street

د.إ 3 AED

Saturday to Thursday from 8:30 to 20:30 and Friday from 14:30 to 20:30.

www.visitdubai.com/en/pois/dubai-museum

Located in the Al Fahidi Fort, the oldest existing fort in Dubai, the Dubai Museum is a great way to explore artefacts from the area and to also learn about Arabian culture and tradition. Every step you take around the museum will have you intrigued and wanting to explore further.

Visitors can exploit the minds of experts who make a living by offering interesting facts and stories about historical events in the area. By the end of the Dubai Museum experience, visitors will be rich with knowledge of Dubai's history and the different people and civilizations that have come across the area.

The museum is both impressive and vast in size and contains a whole host of dioramas, artefacts and exhibits that give a true insight to the daily life in Dubai long before the discovery of oil and the riches that ensued.

There are many galleries that recreate scenes such as mosques, Souks, the old pearling industry and the desert.

The artefacts from the historic pearling industry form one of the most popular exhibits on display. The range includes real equipment such as a set of pearl merchants weights and scales. Visitors will also gain an authentic insight in to just how much Dubai has changed and developed in recent years which will be sure to have you stunned.

Visiting the Dubai Museum and the Al Fahidi Fort is a must do activity for visitors interested in seeking to fulfill their cultural needs and the whole experience will certainly not disappoint.

The Grand Mosque

Al Fahidi

Ali Bin Abi Taleb Street

The Grand Mosque located in Bur Dubai, is one of the most impressive mosques in the UAE and is very much the crown on top of the historical Bur Dubai area. The mosque is of stunning architecture and features the tallest minaret in Dubai measuring at over 70 meters tall.

The mosque was first constructed in the early 1900s but encountered problems in the 60s which subsequently meant that the mosque was torn down and rebuilt.

With a capacity of over 1,000 people, the mosque is one of the biggest and most influential mosques in Dubai and is regarded as the main point of Dubai's religious and cultural life.

Although it is prohibited for non-Muslims to enter the mosque itself, tourists are allowed to enter the minaret from where a good view of Bur Dubai can be seen.

Despite non-Muslim tourists being prohibited from enter the mosque, it is still a popular attraction. Many tourists come to view the impressive architecture behind the building and to take pictures for a lasting memory.

Shiva Hindu Temple

Al Ghubaiba | +971 4 353 5334 | Bur Dubai

The Shiva Temple was built in 1960 and is the only Hindu temple in the city. The temple was originally granted permission by the then ruler of Dubai Sheikh Rashid Al Maktoum in recognition to the vast amount of Indian workers in the city.

Dubai's success is often credited to workers who came from India to build vital infrastructure. At the time, the Indian workers complained that they had nowhere to worship and it was Rashid Al Maktoum who listened and granted them their wish.

The temple is always busy, and even more on a Saturday catering for the 3 million Indians estimated to be living today in Dubai.

Hindus visiting Dubai can worship at the temple while non-worshippers can also enter certain parts of the building to take in the atmosphere.

Saint Mary's Catholic Church

Oud Metha

+971 4 337 0087

Oud Metha Street

Free

Daily from 05:00 to 21:30

saintmarysdubai.org

St. Mary's Catholic Church located opened in 1967 to cater to the needs of the growing Western population who were Catholics. It was an unprecedented milestone that the ruler Sheikh Rashid bin Saeed Al Maktoum gave permission for a Catholic church to be built. It was also one of the first statements of Dubai's intentions to grow and expand into a multicultural city.

The church is an extremely peaceful place yet can accommodate almost 2000 worshippers. Every Saturday, when it is most busy, there is also a canteen offering refreshments and light snacks.

From Monday to Thursday there are four Masses held in English, while on Friday, Saturday and Sunday there are more. There are also masses held in other languages including Arabic, French and Portuguese. For the exact times, please visit the church's website.

Dining

Asha's
Nearest Station: *Dubai Healthcare City*
Address: Pyramids, *WAFI Mall, Oud Metha Road*
Opening Hours: *12:30 to 15:00 and 19:30 to 0:00.*
Phone: *+971 4 324 4100*
Website: *www.ashasrestaurants.com/dubai*

Asha's is one of the most exclusive and best Indian cuisine restaurants in Dubai. The restaurant is owned and named after Asha Bhosle, a renowned Hindi singer and actress.

Asha herself has had a major influence on every aspect of the restaurant including decoration and more prominently, the menu. She has collaborated with chefs to ensure a wide menu that includes Indian classic, in addition to more modern and unique dishes. The menu is impressive and is accompanied with a thorough explanation stating the influences and history of specific dishes.

Asha's is very popular among the large Indian population which is a great sign of authenticity.

Highlights of the menu are the papdi chat with crispy discs layered with yoghurt and chutney, the dhaniya murg and the mirch baingan ka salan complement with a sauce and chunks of young eggplant and coconut.

Asha's is without doubt one of the best places to dine out in Dubai, and you won't be disappointed with the seductive and romantic ambience that it offers.

Yakitori Tei
Nearest Station: *Dubai Healthcare City*
Address: *Ascot Hotel, Bur Dubai*
Opening Hours: *12:30 to 15:00 and 19:30 to 0:00.*
Phone: +97043520900
Website: *www.khamashospitality.com/Ascothotel*

Located in the affluent Ascot Hotel, Yakitori Tei is a mid-range restaurant which specializes in both Thai and Japanese cuisine. The restaurant is extremely inviting with the dark decor and furnishings offering both a warm and comfortable atmosphere.

On entrance, you will be greeted with some background on the restaurant and then be escorted you to your table. You will see many Japanese diners reflecting the quality and authenticity of the food. Diners can also see the chefs in action with the impressive open kitchen.

The menu is extensive and offers something for everyone and portions are large. The highlights of the menu and the most popular dishes are the sashimi and the succulent and tender gyoza dish.

Hotels

Movenpick Hotel, Bur Dubai
Nearest Station: *Dubai Healthcare City*
Address: *19th Street*
Phone: *+971 4 336 6000*
Website: *www.movenpick.com/Dubai*

The five-star Movenpick Hotel is the flagship accommodation in the area and offers a whole range of top class facilities.

The rooms have an elegant design perfectly complemented by the expensive designer furniture. One of their best features is the full length windows which allow for lots of daylight to enter and glorious views of the hotel grounds and the Bur Dubai area. The hotel offers both rooms and apartments to cater for the everybody's needs.

The large apartments come fitted with a fully equipped kitchen and dining table, while a washing machine is also included.

There are a number of fine dining options to choose from including restaurants specializing Arabian, Indian and International cuisines. Night time options include various bars and the popular Pulse nightclub is the perfect option. Other facilities include a fully equipped fitness center, large outdoor swimming pool and a free shuttle bus to Jumeirah Beach.

Majestic Hotel Tower Dubai
Nearest Station: *Al Fahidi*
Address: *Plot No. 317-106, Mankhool Road*
Phone: *+971 4 359 8888*
Website: *www.dubaimajestic.com*

Located in the heart of Bur Dubai, this four-star hotel offers spectacular views over the skyline of the city. Being centrally located, the hotel is only a short walking distance away from a number of top attractions and landmarks.

The rooms at the hotel are all spacious with a fashionable finish. The beds are comfortable with sheets made from the finest fabric. The biggest highlight of the rooms are the luxurious bathrooms with a rain shower, a large bathtub and elegant design. The rooms also include high speed internet, flat screen TVs with international channels, a desk, a mini-bar, international newspapers and 24-hour room service.

In addition to guests being able to lounge on the terrace next to the outdoor swimming pool, all culinary needs are also catered for with seven restaurants on-site. Included in the list is the award winning Elia restaurant which offers the very best in Greek cuisine.

Guests not wanting to leave the pool area can always take advantage of the very strategically placed Tirquaz Garden Lounge which is located right next to the pool and serves Arabian cuisines, as well as shisha.

Hotel guests can also take advantage of the health club featuring sauna and massage treatments while for those wanting a bit of sun, there is a free shuttle bus going to and from the beach on a frequent basis.

Dubai Marina

The fabulous Dubai Marina area is littered with tall and will have you thinking that you are in a city like New York and not in the middle of the desert.

The Dubai Marina development started in 2003 and was one of the major aspects of Dubai's elaborate plan to become one of the most recognizable and popular cities in the world.

What makes it even more remarkable is that the two-mile long shoreline development was all constructed on an artificial island. The eye catching marina is completely man-made and is the location of the famous Jumeirah Beach Walk which offers an array of boutiques, handicraft shops, cafes, restaurants and even an open air cinema all along the waterfront promenade.

When the second half of the development is finished in the years to come, it is estimated that Dubai Marina will house over 120,000 residents in a mix of budget and luxury high-rise homes.

During your stay, a visit to Dubai Marina is a must. The atmosphere is cosmopolitan and the miles of shoreline and public walkways make for relaxing and satisfying of strolls.

The area has an array of architectural styles to see and a whole host of attractions and entertainment options to exploit.

Attractions

Marina Beach

Jumeirah Beach Residence (Tram) | د.إ Free

Marina Beach is one of the most beautiful and popular beaches in Dubai with hordes of tourists and residents flocking there every day to enjoy and make the most of the white sands and the warm waters.

Located in the relatively new Dubai Marina area of the city, Marina Beach is the best place to top up your tan while still being near a range of restaurants and drink and ice cream vendors.

When visiting the beach, you will be able to see just how well the city has blended its modern and elaborate infrastructure to the natural beauties that existed long before the expansive development.

The beach is extremely popular among families with facilities such as baby changing rooms, children's playgrounds and shade areas.

In addition, the beach is perfect for playing traditional beach games. There are also workers on the beach hiring out sunbeds by the hour for a reasonable price. Showers are located on the promenade next to the beach.

Dubai Marina Walk

Marina Towers (Tram)	د.إ Free
Open 24/7.	www.dubai-marina.com

The Dubai Marina Walk is without A doubt one of the most beautiful walks in Dubai and it will have you catered for the entire day. The total length of the walk is roughly 4.5 miles (7 km).

To keep you enticed and entertained along your way round, in addition to breathtaking views of the surrounding areas and the beautiful Persian Gulf, the beachfront walkway has over 300 outlets along the way! The stores offer everything from fashion items to jewelry to handmade goods and much more.

One of the most popular and affluent shopping areas on the walk is at the Convent Garden Market where vendors sell beautiful handmade jewelry, clothing and artisan produced souvenirs for the perfect memory of your visit.

A choice of over 70 restaurants and cafes will also keep you fresh with the majority of these offering a beautiful coastal view for the ultimate relaxation period after a spot of shopping.

The restaurants located on the Dubai Marina Walk offer a wide range of international and local dishes to cater for all tastes and for people of all backgrounds and ages so you will be sure to find something that takes your fancy.

When walking the route, visitors are treated to and entertained by an array of public events.

The most popular area for street entertainers is in the Cobblestone Boulevard part of the walk.

The Cobblestone Boulevard is often extremely busy so for those wishing to avoid large crowds, then it is recommended to visit during the weekdays as opposed to the weekends.

Dubai Marina Yacht Club

Jumeirah Lakes Towers

د.إ Free

+971 4 362 7900

Open 24/7.

Dubai Marina

www.dubaimarinayachtclub.com

The cream on top of the Dubai Marina area, the Dubai Marina Yacht Club just oozes class and exclusivity in one of the most affluent areas of Dubai. The Yacht Club consists of four marinas located in close proximity to one another.

The most luxurious marina is the Club House Marina which stands in the most prominent location out of the four. The clubhouse is the location of two fine dining eateries and the sought after and exclusive cigar lounge.

To further enhance the exclusivity of The Club House Marina, only members are granted with access.

The Dubai Marina Yacht Club also has the facilities to provide the perfect business meeting environment with a large conference center offering room length windows, buffet options, a fully equipped bar and also a beautiful outside terrace.

For those who can afford it, The Dubai Yacht Club charter the use of their luxury yachts. They are large enough to hold up to 14 people and comes with a fully staffed crew and full dining options.

Overall, although the majority of tourists won't be able to get inside of the venue, walking around the marinas will still give you a sense of exclusivity and it is a great opportunity to gain an insight into one of the most elegant locations in the city.

Dubai Marina Mall

Dubai Marina Mall (Tram)

+971 4 436 1020

Sheikh Zayed Road, Dubai

د.إ Free

Saturday to Wednesday from 10:00 to 22:00, Thursday and Friday from 10:00 to 0:00

www.dubaimarinamall.com

Located on the waterfront, the Dubai Marina Mall is one of the largest shopping malls in Dubai.

Featuring four levels, the Dubai Marina Mall covers almost 400,000 square feet with over 130 shopping outlets, numerous restaurants offering cuisines from all over the world, a cinema and also a children's entertainment complex.

The mall is relatively new and comprises of everything expected from a modern and large shopping center. The atmosphere is relaxed and the layout is designed for a spacious and worry-free shopping experience.

Most of the biggest international brands are represented in the mall including Adidas, Nike, Baldi, Aldo, Billabong, Boots Pharmacy, Bobbi Brown, Diesel, Gant, H&M, Zara, Levi's, Mango, River Island, Superdry, Ted Baker and many more.

Dining options are vast with al fresco waterfront dining also a possibility. Restaurants located in the Dubai Marina Mall include Five Guys, GBK, Chickenow, India Palace and Zafran. Fast food outlets such as McDonalds and Subway are also represented in the mall.

Dining

Bussola
Nearest Station: *Mina Seyahi Tram Station*
Address: *The Westin Dubai Mina Seyahi Beach Resort & Marina*
Opening Hours: *12:00 to 14:30 and 17:30 to 23:30*
Phone: *+971 4 399 4141*
Website: *www.bussoladubai.com*

Bussola is a beautiful Italian restaurant located on the waterfront of the magnificent Dubai Marina.

Diners visiting the restaurant will be greeted with two dining options: the first is to secure a table on the upper floor terrace to enjoy pizzas cooked on the wood-fire. From here, diners can enjoy a delightful view of the marina which really enhances the whole dining experience.

Alternatively, diners can also choose to sit in the main section of the restaurant or on the lower level outdoor terrace. If you choose this option, you will then be eligible to eat from main menu.

The restaurant is modern with a beautiful wooden interior. The staff mainly consist of Italian natives so they can really give you a reliable recommendation when it comes to choosing a dish. The pasta is freshly cooked with the highlights of the menu including the potato gnocchi with ossobuco ragu and grana padano cheese, the Seafood Acquerello aged rice risotto and the breaded veal chop with pont neuf potatoes.

Mogador
Nearest Station: *Damac Properties*
Address: *Dubai Marina*
Opening Hours: *18:30 to 23:30*
Phone: *+971 4 450 8520*

Located in relative tranquility away from the busier parts of Dubai Marina, Mogador is a restaurant serving delicious and authentic Moroccan cuisine. One of the highlights of Mogador other than the food is the waterfront view that it can offer. Diners come here to enjoy Moroccan delicacies in a relaxed and chilled out atmosphere.

The food is more affordable than most Dubai Marina restaurants while the quality is on a par with the more exclusive eateries in the area.

The friendly staff are on hand to offer recommendations on the dishes available to ensure you are comfortable with what you are ordering. The highlight of the menu is the seafood, which is fresh straight off the boat.

Hotels

The Address, Dubai Marina
Nearest Station: *Dubai Marina Mall Tram*
Address: *Dubai Marina*
Phone: *+971 4 436 7777*
Website: *www.theaddress.com*

By far one of the most expensive, exclusive and well known hotels in the Dubai Marina area, The Address will have their guests in awe.

Not only does it offer the most perfect of locations, the facilities on offer are second to none. The staff strive to give you celebrity treatment and the building itself is just enormous.

The five-star hotel has a number of different room options, but even the most basic rooms will have you feeling like royalty. All rooms offer spectacular views looking over Dubai Marina and will have you dazing out of the window all day. All rooms come with flat screen TVs equipped with satellite channels, an iPod dock, high speed internet access, a minibar, coffee and tea making facilities and 24-hour room service.

When not enjoying in the modern and elegant rooms, the hotel has you well catered for in other areas. For guests wanting to take a dip, they can enjoy the rooftop infinity pool with breathtaking views over Dubai Marina. To unwind after a long day, guests can take advantage of the large spa which offers numerous treatments and massages. The hotel also features a gym.

Also on site are a range of luxury restaurants specializing in Asian, European and Arabic cuisine. Guests can then head over to one of the many bars and enjoy an alcoholic beverage and atmosphere of their choice.

Sheraton Jumeirah Beach Resort
Nearest Station: *Dubai Marina Mall Tram*
Address: *Al Sufouh Road*
Phone: *+971 4 399 5533*
Website: *www. sheratonjumeirahbeach.com*

The fabulous Sheraton Jumeirah Beach Resort hotel is located on a private beach on the Dubai Marina. The location is an absolute dream for any guests wishing for a stay right on the beachside.

Guests also have exclusive access to the beach at any time they wish.

The five-star hotel features a range of high class facilities on site such an impressive outdoor pool surrounded with comfortable sun-loungers, a fully equipped gym with personal trainers and even tennis and squash courts for those who wish to keep active during their stay.

Guests can also exploit the Armonia spa located on site which offers a number of beauty treatments, steam rooms and saunas.

Rooms feature modern decor and all come with flat screen TVs, large bathroom, coffee and tea maker and also a fully stocked minibar. For those who are lucky enough, some of the rooms even feature views of the coast.

Located in the resort is also a variety of classy restaurants specializing in Asian, Indian, Arabic and European cuisine.

Jebel Ali

Jebel Ali is located 22 miles southwest of Dubai and is one of the largest free trade zones in the world. The free trade zone was established in 1985 and it was designed to bring foreign investment to the area to further go ambitious expansion plans designed for the city of Dubai.

The Jebel Ali area has become a leading provider of sustainable industrial and logistics infrastructure solutions. Today, there are over 7000 companies from all over the world operating in the area.

The biggest feature of Jebel Ali area is the port, which is the largest man made port in the world. Built in 1979, the port has grown to become the busiest port in the Middle East delivering and receiving cargo from over 120 countries.

Another highlight of the area is the Palm Jebel Ali, which is an artificial island in the same shape as Palm Jumeirah. The construction began in 2002, but due to the recent global financial crisis, construction has been put on hold due to lack of investment.

The chairman of the project remains committed to the project and expects construction to resume in the coming years. Once complete, Palm Jebel Ali will be 50% larger than Palm Jumeirah and house over 250,000 people.

Attractions

Gurunanak Darbar Sikh Temple

Energy	www.gurudwaradubai.com
+971 4 882 7550	Jebel Ali, Al Muntazah

The Gurunanak Darbar Sikh Temple is something of true beauty and a must see for visitors.

Built in 2010, it was originally built to accommodate the 50,000 people of the Sikh faith living in the city of Dubai.

It was the first Gurunanak Temple to be built in the area and even received help from the ruler of Dubai who granted a Dubai based Sikh industrialist permission to build the temple on private land.

The temple has the capacity to hold over 600 worshippers with special prayers taking place every Friday.

Other than for special prayers, the temple is also used for solemnizing marriages and holding other religious ceremonies.

For visitors of the Sikh faith, it is possible to join in the special prayers, while non-worshippers are still allowed into the building to see the impressive interior and if you're lucky enough, you will even be able to observe Sikhs practicing their religion.

Dining

White Orchid
Nearest Station: *Jafza Metro Station*
Address: *JA Palm Tree Court, Lobby Level, Dubai*
Opening Hours: *06:30 to 11:00 and 18:30 to 23:00.*
Phone: *+971 4 814 5555*
Website: *www.jaresortshotels.com*

White Orchid is located close to the entrance bridge of the Palm Jebel Ali and specializes in South Asian cuisine. It is a mix between a restaurant and a lounge with most people heading on to the lounge area once they have finished their meal. Once in the lounge, guests can take advantage of the full service bar and live music.

The interior is vastly modern with South Asian influences and the large terrace area features a beautiful view over the JA Palm Tree Court resort where it is located. The restaurant is certainly a place which makes it easy to unwind and relax and the romantic ambience makes for the perfect date location.

The food is flavorsome and represents a true vision of South Asia. The highlights of the menu include the crispy prawn & black sesame tempura, the slow roasted pork belly served with prune, chili and coriander puree, and also the panko-garlic chicken and black truffle which will certainly have you licking your lips.

Accommodation

JA Jebel Ali Beach Hotel
Nearest Station: *Jafza Metro Station*
Address: *Exit No 13, Sheikh Zayed, Free Zone*
Phone: *+971 4 814 5555*
Website: *www.jaresortshotels.com*

Situated overlooking the Persian Gulf and the 18-hole Jebel Ali Golf Resort, the five-star JA Jebel Ali Beach Hotel is very much the flagship hotel in the Jebel Ali area.

The resort is beautiful with guests able to access the private white sanded beach at any time. The outdoor pool area is also a prominent feature of the hotel with sun loungers and palm trees making for the perfect relaxation area.

The rooms are all furnished in a modern style with elegant furniture and full length windows allowing for the room to be lit up. The rooms also have a large balcony allowing for views of the coast and the resort gardens.

All rooms include a flat screen TV with international channels, international newspapers, and a separate seating area. The bathroom is also modern with a rain shower and large tub.

Facilities provided by the hotel are vast and include a fitness center, a modern spa with a range of treatments, hot tubs, saunas, sailing, windsurfing and also tennis courts. Guests can also enjoy a round of golf in a beautiful setting with shuttle buses running to and from the course.

There is also a kids club to keep the little ones entertained while you take advantage of the world class facilities.

Further Afield

Some attractions that are worth seeing are not in any of the areas that we have covered thus far.

This section includes some of these other locations that you may want to visit during your time in Dubai.

Attractions

Emirates Towers

Emirates Towers

www.jumeirah.com/Emirates-Towers

+971 4 330 0000

Sheikh Zayed Rd

Located in the business district of Dubai, the Emirates Towers consist of The Emirates Office Tower and the Jumeirah Emirates Towers Hotel.

The Emirates Office Tower is the taller of the two standing at 355 meters tall and as of 2016 is the 23rd tallest building in the world. The Emirates Towers Hotel stands at 309 meters tall and is currently the 47th tallest building in the world.

The towers are an acclaimed part of the city and the enormous size of the buildings mean that they are a popular attraction for visitors.

The whole complex is complete with a large number of gardens, lakes and waterfalls for visitors to enjoy a relaxed stroll while admiring the towers.

There is also a retail development known as the Boulevard for visitors to enjoy a spot of retail therapy during their stop in the area.

Dubai Parks and Resorts

Jebel Ali + taxi for 15km

د.إ See description.

+971 4 820 0000

Hours vary seasonally and by park.

Sheik Zayed Rd,
Opposite Palm Jebel Ali

www.dubaiparksandresorts.com

Dubai Parks and Resorts is the region's largest integrated theme park resort - consisting of three theme parks and one water park. The complex opened in October 2016.

As part of the resort, guests can explore Motiongate Dubai, Bollywood Parks Dubai, LEGOLAND Dubai and LEGOLAND Water Park. There are over 100 attractions in total.

The destination also features a central plaza area with dining and shopping called Riverland Dubai and an on-site hotel called Lapita Hotel Dubai.

The Motiongate theme park features areas dedicated to Sony Pictures, a Smurfs Village area, an indoor Dreamworks area, as well as another dedicated to Lionsgate movies. A one-day ticket is priced at 280 AED for children and 330 for AED adults.

Bollywood Parks will have zones themed to studios, Mumbai, a royal palace and a rustic ravine. Tickets for one day are 245 AED per child and 265 per adult.

LEGOLAND Dubai will feature all things toy related and even has an added water park.

The parks are targeted at ages 2 to 12. Theme park prices are 250 AED for kids and 295 AED for adults. The water park is 240 AED for adults and 200 AED for kids.

A single admission ticket for all theme parks is also available - pricing for 2 days is 650 AED for kids and 730 AED for adults, 3 days is 765 AED and 870 AED and 4 days is 790 AED and 890 AED respectively.

A 2-day, 1 park per day ticket is also available at 450 AED for kids and 530 for adults. Annual passes are also available.

Big Red

The Big Red offers visitors the chance to experience numerous adrenaline-filled activities in the desert dunes such as 4x4 rides, dirt biking, quad biking and sandboarding. The encounter is sure to get the heart racing and you will be left with a desert experience of a lifetime.

There are a few tour companies heading to the dunes a few times per day but they are often full so it is recommended to book your place in advance.

On the way to the dunes, the bus will stop on a street where there are companies who hire out quad bikes, 4x4's and sandboards and allow you to curb your adrenaline junkie needs. A fantastic and mesmerizing experience!

Dubai World Trade Centre

Metro	World Trade Centre	Address	Sheikh Zayed Road
Phone	+971 4 332 1000	Website	www.dwtc.com

Built in 1978, the Dubai World Trade Center in the modern day isn't just at the forefront of the city's business interests, but it has also become an attraction for hundreds of thousands of visitors each year.

Vast in size, the whole complex consists of the trade center itself, eight large exhibition halls, a residence complex and also the Dubai International Convention Center.

Visitors to the World Trade Center are permitted to look around the buildings although some exhibitions may be subject to an entrance fee. Visit the website to check for events and exhibitions happening on-site.

Dubai Butterfly Garden

Miracle Garden (Bus)

د.إ 30 AED per person

+971 4 332 1000

Daily from 9:00 to 18:00.

Al Barsha South 3, By Dubai Miracle Garden

www.dubaibutterflygarden.com

Both a fantastic and rare experience, the newly opened Dubai Butterfly Garden is the first of its kind in the Middle East.

Comprising over 1,800 square meters, the garden features nine domes in which features thousands of different butterfly species from all over the world are housed.

In addition to the domes, there is also a butterfly flower garden and butterfly museum on-site to gain an extensive insight of these beautiful and elegant creatures.

Visiting the Dubai Butterfly Garden is especially popular with families and makes for a great day out.

Dubai Sports City

Sports City (Bus)	Varies by event.
+971 4 425 1111	Varies by event.
Sheikh Mohammed Bin Zayed Rd	www.dubaisportscity.ae

Opened in 2008, Dubai Sports City is the most renowned and popular area of Dubai dedicated to the hosting of sporting events; the area also houses numerous sporting academies.

Dubai Sports City often hosts international sporting fixtures along with the occasional music concert.

The multi-venue sports complex has a total area of over 15,000,000 meters squared with the most distinguished feature of the complex being the Dubai International Cricket Stadium which has a capacity of 25,000 people.

The stadium hosts international cricket fixtures in the cooler winter months.

In addition to the cricket stadium, there is also a stadium dedicated to Rugby which is called Rugby Park and features a seating capacity of 5,000 people. An 18-hole golf course is also located on the complex and was designed by famous professional golfer Ernie Els.

Academies operating from the venue include the ICC Cricket Academy, Spanish Soccer Schools led by former Real Madrid player Michel Salgado, a Rugby Academy, Swimming Academy and also a Golf Academy.

Dubai Tennis Stadium

Dubai Civil Aviation College (Bus)

+971 4 282 4122

Garhoud, Dubai

د.إ Varies by event.

Varies by event.

www.dubaidutyfreetennischampionships.com

The Dubai Duty Free Tennis Stadium is the biggest tennis stadium in Dubai and home to the ATP 500 Series Dubai Duty Free Tennis Championships. The tournament is a big draw and attracts capacity crowds especially with some of the biggest names in professional tennis competing at the tournament.

The stadium is modern and with a vibrant atmosphere, especially when the stadium is full to the 5,000 capacity.

In addition to the stadium during competition time, the tennis village is full of exciting things to keep you entertained and amused. There are also numerous restaurants and pubs open all year round to keep you well refreshed.

When not hosting tennis events, the stadium is used to host the occasional music concert with past acts including Madonna, Bryan Adams and Sting. Even when there is no event on, the area is still a popular place to visit.

Seasonal Events

As if you needed yet another reason to visit Dubai, the city hosts exciting seasonal events throughout the year. Many of these are regular fixtures that visitors return for year after year. This chapter covers some of the biggest temporary events each year.

January

Dubai Shopping Festival - 26th Dec 2016 to 28th Jan 2017

Held at the start of the year, the Dubai Shopping Festival attracts countless visitors to the city each year looking to take advantage of the vast price reductions offered by stores.

Globally known as a shopping haven, visitors to the city during this period can take advantage of the large shopping malls and independent stores in order to grab a bargain.

The festival is also a course for celebration with numerous events around the city such as fireworks, music concerts and children's entertainment providing the perfect backdrop after a hard day of shopping.

Website: http://www.visitdubai.com/en/events/dubai-shopping-festival-2017

McLaren Cup - 19th Jan to 2nd Feb 2017

Part of the Dubai Polo Series, 2017 will see the eighth edition of the McLaren Cup take place.

Being sponsored by McLaren, the event is also the perfect place to spot a few supercars and enjoy music from international DJs.

The event will take place at Al Habtoor Polo Resort and Club (telephone: +971 56 373 2999)

With no spectator fees, this is one polo championship that is open to people from all backgrounds, rich or poor.

One of the most respectable tournaments of its kind around the world, the McLaren Cup is sure to please lovers of the sport.

Website: www.dubaipologoldcup.com

Dubai Marathon - 20th January 2017

The yearly Dubai Marathon attracts a host of visitors to the city hoping to finish the scenic route and ultimately raise some money for charity.

The event hosts over 25,000 runners every year including the very best marathon athletes in the world.

The whole atmosphere during marathon day can be compared to a carnival one with many people dressed up in costumes in an attempt to raise as much money for their chosen charity as possible.

Whether you are running, supporting or just a bystander, this is a unique atmosphere that should be experienced if you are in the city in January.

Website: www.dubaimarathon.org

February

Dubai Desert Classic - 30th January to 5th February 2017

Hosted by the beautiful Emirates Golf Club, the yearly Dubai Desert Classic attracts some of the best golfers to the city in addition to a large number of visitors hoping to see their hero's in action.

It is by far the most prestigious golf tournament held in the city, and is always entertaining.

Website: www.dubaidesertclassic.com

Dubai International Jazz Festival - 22nd to 24th February 2017

Held in the Dubai Media City area of the city, the Dubai International Jazz Festival is one of the most vibrant and eagerly anticipated events hosted by the city.

The atmosphere is relaxed with visitors traveling from all over the world to see some of the world's most known Jazz artists do their thing.

Website: www.dubaijazzfest.com

Dubai Tennis Championships - 19th Feb to 4th March 2017

One of the most prestigious and famous sporting events to enlighten the city, the Dubai Tennis Championships is contested by the top players in the sport and always attracts a full capacity crowd.

The impressive Dubai Duty Free Tennis stadium is the stage for the final with the whole surrounding village providing entertainment, luxury cuisine and a vibrant atmosphere.

Website: www.dubaidutyfreetennischampionships.com

March

Art Dubai - 15th to 18th March 2017

The Art Dubai festival is a must-see attraction for anyone who even remotely has an interest in art.

Artists flock from all over the world in order to showcase their abilities with the festival drawing a wide range of innovative work. The festival is split into three styles: contemporary, modern and marker.

Website: www.artdubai.ae

Dubai World Cup - 25th March 2017

Home to the richest horse race on planet earth, the Dubai World Cup is one of the most highly contested horse races of the year with the very best horses, jockeys and trainers vying to take home a share of the $10 million U.S. prize fund.

The race is especially popular with spectators wanting to indulge in a day of luxury at the state-of-the-art Meydan Racecourse.

Website: www.dubaiworldcup.com

Dubai Food Festival - 9th to 11th March 2017

One of the most anticipated events of the year for all food lovers, the Festival of Taste brings together some of the world's best chefs who demonstrate and give invaluable tips on how to cook the meal of your dreams.

In addition to the chefs, there are exhibitions showcasing the very best cuisine from around the world including local dishes.

Website: www.tasteofdubaifestival.com

April

UAE Desert Challenge - 1st to 7th April 2017

A sporting event that leaves the city for the desert, the UAE Desert Challenge is one part of FIA Cross Country Rally World Cup and provides some adrenaline pumping entertainment.

The rally begins in neighboring Abu Dhabi before finishing in the Dubai desert over a five day period.

This is the ideal entertainment for petrol heads.

Website: www.abu dhabidesert challenge.com

May

Dubai Tango Festival - 2017 dates to be confirmed

Usually spanning four days, The Dubai Tango Festival event is a chance to learn and practice your dance moves with live music each and every night.

A gala dinner and the fact the event supports a charity makes this all the more special.

Website: www. tangodubai.org

June to August

Dubai Summer Surprises - 2017 dates to be confirmed

Celebrating its 20th year in 2017, Dubai Summer Surprises is a shopping extravaganza with live music performances, large discounts from shops and extended opening hours at selected shopping malls.

The Big Summer Sale part of the festival is particularly well-attended, providing luxury branded goods at more accessible prices.

Website: www.visitdubai.com/en/dss

September to November

Dubai Music Week - 2017 dates to be confirmed

Much fans can rejoice as Dubai becomes the center of the music world for one week each September.

As well as live acts and concerts, you can expect classes and celebrity speakers to be present. The event takes place at the Dubai World Trade Center.

Website: www.dubaimusicweek.ae

December

Dubai Rugby Sevens - 30th November to 2nd December 2016

Especially popular with visitors from Great Britain, Australia and New Zealand, as well as locals, the Dubai Rugby Sevens is one of the biggest sporting events to descend upon the city every year.

The 3-day competition features 16 of the top ranked international rugby teams locked in battle to take home the coveted trophy.

2017 dates are yet to be announced.

Website: www.dubairugby7s.com

National Day Festival - 1st to 3rd December

The national day and the biggest celebration of the calendar, the National Day Festival commemorates Dubai gaining their independence from Great Britain.

Celebrated on 2nd December each year, visitors in the city at the time will be able to take advantage of special events and also free entry to some of the most renowned landmarks in the city.

On 1st December in anticipation of the main day, the "National Day Arabic Concerts" featuring Emirati artists take place in the city.

Website: www.visitdubai.com/en

Dubai International Film Festival - 7th to 14th December 2016

One of the flagship annual festivals held in the city, the Dubai International Film Festival features a host of independently made films from all over the world, as well as nationally produced films, documentaries and of course the Hollywood blockbusters.

Visitors are attracted by not only the films, but also the Hollywood stars who are present during the festival.

Website: www.dubaifilmfest.com

A Special Thanks

If you have made it this far, thank you very much for reading everything. We hope this guide will make a big difference to your trip to Dubai! Remember to take this guide with you while you are visiting this amazing place.

If you have any questions or wish to contact us, you can do so at www.independentguidebooks.com/contact-us/. If you have any corrections, feedback about any element of the guide, or a review of an attraction, hotel, area or restaurant – send us a message and we will get back to you.

We also encourage you to leave a review on Amazon's website, or wherever you have purchased this guide from. Your reviews make a huge difference in helping other people find this guide, and we really appreciate your help.

If you have enjoyed this guide, other travel guides in this series include:

- The Independent Guide to New York City
- The Independent Guide to Paris
- The Independent Guide to London
- The Independent Guide to Hong Kong
- The Independent Guide to Universal Orlando
- The Independent Guide to Disneyland
- The Independent Guide to Disneyland Paris
- The Independent Guide to Walt Disney World
- The Independent Guide to Universal Studios Hollywood

Have a fantastic time in Dubai!

Photo Credits:

Used under a Creative Commons license:
Intro sunset and neighbourhoods page sunset - the_dead_pixel; Dubai creek in history section -Christiane Birr; Dirhams - Tour Fethi; Oil - Sergio Russo; UAE Flag - Abdulla Al Muchairi; Dubai Skyline - Iam_chihang; Climate desert photo - worldinframes; Population photo in mall - Jay Galvin; Jumeirah mosque in religion section - Gavin; Tip Sign - Colin Davis; Man and women looking over water in traditional clothes - Michael Coghlan; Living Room in House - Sarah Ackerman; Shake Shack Ramadan Sign - Krista; Cocktail - Adrian Scottow; FlyDubai - Hugh Llewelyn; Emirates Express Buses - Achilli Family; Abu dhabi Airport Interior - Travpacker.com; Nol Card - sightseeingguy.com; Tram, Jumeirah Beach and Yacht Club - Guilhem Vellut; Monorail - Tim Adams; Bus - Michiel; Abra - Ryan Lackey; Highway - Vijay Chennupati; Burj al Arab neighbourhood page - brando.n; Jumeirah Mosque - Susanne Nilsson; Wild Wadi Water Park - Sarah Ackerman; Aquarium - Masaru Kamikura; Dubai Zoo - Shahid Ahmed Siddiqi; Dubai Creek - Christ Combe; Deira Clocktower - Mohamed Nazmi; Gold Souk - Paul Fenwick; Dhow Wharfage - 'bettyx1138'; Mamzar Beach Park - travelourplanet.com; Downtown Dubai - Sonya Bobb; Burj Khalifa - Hisham Binsuwaif; Dubai Fountain - Roman Emin; Dubai Mall Waterfall - Steven Straiton; Bastakia Quarter - McKay Savage; Creekside Park - Kathrin Mezger; Dubai Museum - Alan Davey; The Grand Mosque - Step; Dubai Marina - Fabio Achilli; Marina Beach - Anand Khatri; Marina Walk - Francisco Anzola; Dubai Marina Mall - bettyx1138; emirate's towers - Book Blagoev; Big Red - Bryn Pinzgauer; Dubai Butterfly Garden - Oiva Eskola; UAE Desert Challenge - HIMOINSA Racing Team; Taste of Dubai and Rugby Sevens - Land Rovers MENA;

Cover - Burj Khalifa - MNMagic; skyline - junie_alaan; Mosque - Florian Martys; Burj Al Arab - brando.n; Atlantis - Alberto-g-rovi; Historic part - Mathias Apitz; Pots - Muhammad Ahmed; Madinat Jumeirah - Djordje Radovanovic

Additional images (non-Creative Commons) from: Photo of table by sea - Flooka; Location - DBXMarine.com; Al Ahmadiya School - Culture Arts (Wikipedia); Golf Club - alldubai.ae; Al Dawaar - hyattrestaurants.com; Social House Restaurant - myfashdiary.com; Dubai Dolphinarium - raynatours.com; Asha's - Pyramidrestaurantsatwafi.com; Bussola - bussoladubai.com; Gurunanak Darbar Sikh Temple - thenational.ae; Jebel Ali - adgeco.com; Dubai Parks and Resorts - constructionweekonline.com; Dubai Sports City - propsearch.ae; Shopping Festival, Dubai Summer Surprises and McLaren Cup - visitdubai.com; Tennis Championships - dubaidutyfreetennischampionships.com; Dubai Tango - viewsatelier.com;

19979392R00055

Printed in Great Britain
by Amazon